MARVEL STUDIOS

SPIDER-MAN
No Way Home

"With Great Power Comes Great Responsibility."

With his secret identity exposed following the events of *Spider-Man: Far From Home*, Peter Parker asks Doctor Strange to cast a spell to make the world forget who he really is. But when the spell goes wrong, the Multiverse is laid open, allowing villains from other universes through to menace our hero. When two other Spider-Men also arrive, Peter finds himself at the center of an epic adventure like nothing he has ever experienced before.

THE OFFICIAL MARVEL STUDIOS SPECIALS

Thor: Ragnarok
Black Panther
Black Panther: The Official Movie Companion
Marvel Studios: The First 10 Years
Avengers: Infinity War
Ant-Man and The Wasp
Captain Marvel
Avengers: Endgame
Avengers: An Insider's Guide to the Avengers Films
Black Widow
WandaVision
The Falcon and the Winter Soldier
Eternals
Loki
Doctor Strange in the Multiverse of Madness

TITAN EDITORIAL
Editor Jonathan Wilkins
Group Editor Jake Devine
Art Director Oz Browne
Editorial Assistant Calum Collins
Copy Editor Matt McAllister
Production Controller Kelly Fenlon
Production Controller Caterina Falqui
Production Manager Jackie Flook
Sales and Circulation Manager Steve Tothill
Marketing Coordinator Lauren Noding
Publicity and Sales Coordinator Alexandra Iciek
Publicity Manager Will O'Mullane
Digital and Marketing Manager Jo Teather
Publishing Directors Ricky Claydon
& John Dziewiatkowski
Group Operations Director Alex Ruthen
Executive Vice President Andrew Sumner
Publishers Vivian Cheung & Nick Landau

DISTRIBUTION
U.S. Distribution: Penguin Random House
U.K. Distribution: MacMillan Distribution
Direct Sales Market: Diamond Comic Distributors
General Inquiries:
customerservice@titanpublishingusa.com

PRINTED IN CHINA

Marvel Studios' Spider-Man No Way
Home The Official Movie Special published
February 2023 by Titan Magazines, a division of Titan
Publishing Group Limited, 144 Southwark Street,
London, SE1 0UP.

For sale in the U.S. and Canada.

ISBN: 9781787737181

Thanks to, Kevin Pearl,
Samantha Keane, Shiho Tilley.
and Eugene Paraszczuk at Disney.

CONTENTS

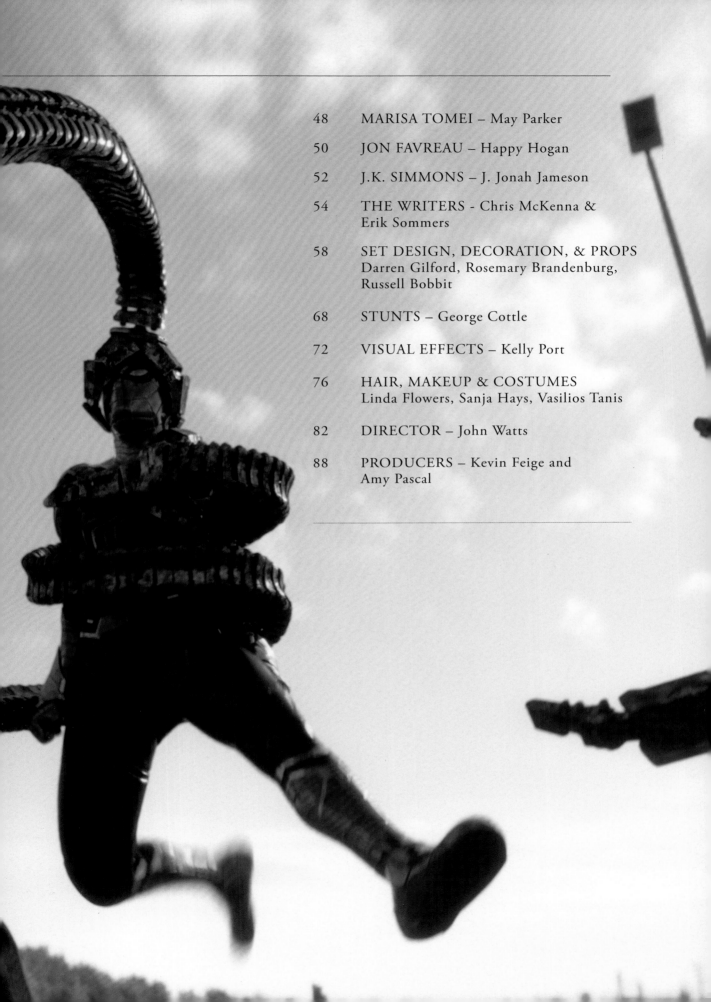

TOM HOLLAND

TOM HOLLAND
PETER PARKER/
SPIDER-MAN

Tom Holland is back in the dual role of Peter Parker and Spider-Man – but this time he's joined by two other web-slingers. The actor discusses what the earlier Spidey movies meant to him and reveals why *No Way Home*'s stunts are bigger and better than ever before.

PUBLIC ENEMY #1

01 Tom Holland strikes a pose as Peter Parker, your friendly neighborhood Spider-Man!

02 The action begins seconds after the coda of *Spider-Man: Far from Home,* with Peter exposed to the world as Spider-Man.

03 Peter finds life even harder when everybody knows his secret.

04 Peter's attempt to secure a place at MIT is put on hold!

05 Doc Ock gets a grip on Peter... just not the Peter he was expecting!

06 A wounded Peter Parker fights on.

What came into your mind when you heard that Tobey Maguire and Andrew Garfield were joining you in *No Way Home*?

I didn't believe it at first. Jon [Watts, director] pitched me the idea and I thought, "That'll never happen. There's no way they'll be able to figure that out. They won't agree to do that, it's just not gonna happen." And here we are! Then we had an amazing [first] day, where we all had our suits on and we all sort of swapped stories about how you put them on, how you take them off, where the zippers are and all that sort of stuff. It was kinda crazy.

The earlier *Spider-Man* films had a big influence on the Super Hero genre, didn't they?

Loads. Those guys are powerhouses. It was amazing for me to be there with them, because I remember going to the cinema to see [Tobey Maguire's] first film and the second one and the third one. And I remember I watched [Andrew Garfield's] first film when I was in Wales shooting a film... I remember saying in an interview years ago that my dream role would be to play Spider-Man. And to be there with those two was mind-blowing. To get to know them both and to sort of bring back this perfect full circle story... I was just honored to be a part of it really.

Did they influence your version of Peter Parker and Spider-Man?
I'm all original me, mate! No, I mean I could talk for hours about it, but I remember seeing both of their films when I was younger and just being so mesmerized by the idea of being Spider-Man. For me, it was taking that childhood dream and putting it into my version. Kind of remembering how it felt as a kid to watch them do it, to remember how excited I was, and to put that into my Peter Parker.

I have seen [Andrew Garfield's] first *Spider-Man* more than any film I've seen in the cinema. I must've seen that film like five times... For me, it was just that quirky ad-libbing that he did, which is so fun. I could talk for ages about it. There's aspects of both of them in my character, but for us it was just about making him as young and as relatable and as sweet and innocent as possible. Because what happens to him is so horrible, it means that he's able to deal with it on a much more personal level. I guess the idea for us was to just make him as relatable as possible so he is every person's Super Hero rather than one type of Super Hero.

It was interesting in rehearsal. [Tobey Maguire] would talk about something that he had clearly thought about while making his movies and [Andrew Garfield] would talk about something that was clearly something he had thought about but I had never thought about. It was so interesting to think about the character in that way. I think about it in my own way, so it was nice to hear their take on the way they would handle a certain situation. ▶

06

TOM'S ORIGINAL AUDITION

Back in 2015, Tom Holland won the role of Spider-Man in *Captain America: Civil War* over the 7,000 other actors who went up for the role. He explained more about his audition and what Spider-Man meant to him…

What was the audition process like?
It was a pretty daunting process, if I'm honest. I mean, I went through a phase of just doing self-tapes after self-tapes after self-tapes. And then I finally did an in-room audition with [casting director] Sarah Finn. Then I did one more self-tape, and after that I did my first take with Robert [Downey Jr.] and then I did my second take with Chris [Evans]. It was really scary the first time, because there were six of us auditioning for the movie. We all met each other and we got to sort of hang out briefly before our auditions and kind of scope each other out and figure out what everyone was about.

You were a big fan of *Spider-Man* before this, weren't you?
Yeah, that's crazy. I was at the *Empire* Awards in London [five years before winning the role], and one of the interviewers asked me if I could be a Super Hero who would I be? And I said, "I'd like to be the Spider-Man after Andrew Garfield." And he said, "Would you do the reboot of the reboot?" And I said, "Yeah, the reboot of the reboot maybe in 10 years' time." I would never have guessed that, first, that would come true and, secondly, come true within five years! So that was a crazy, crazy day for me.

How did it feel to get the role?
I mean, my journey with Marvel Studios and Sony is too big and too exciting to try and explain in one interview. I don't think I would do it justice. But if you want me to put it in a nutshell, it changed my life. It's been the most extraordinary experience I think anyone could possibly imagine. It's taken me around the world. It's sort of totally opened up a whole new world for me - in our real world and in this crazy world we call the Marvel Cinematic Universe. It's just been the most fulfilling and most exciting thing I think I could've ever imagined.

What did you want to inject into the franchise with *Spider-Man: Homecoming*?
Well, one of the main things that Jon and I really pushed for was to make a new Spider-Man something we hadn't seen before. And the story's set in high school. It's really about a kid trying to deal with doing his homework, asking the girl to the dance, being late for school, but also trying to save New York from this crazy villain. To see that contrast was really interesting… [*Homecoming* is] really fun because Peter Parker is not the finished article. He is constantly learning throughout the movie.

07 Peter unleashes the Iron Spider limbs..-

08 Chaos on the bridge as Spidey tries to save innocent bystanders.

09 Spider-Man slings his web during the climactic confrontation on the Statue of Liberty!

07

08

09

10

"If you want to do a quadruple blackflip over an electric zap
or something, that can happen."

10 Peter and his
amazing friends,
Ned Leeds and MJ.

11 Spider-Man strikes
a familiar pose.

► Were you excited to push the action sequences further
than ever before?
Well, I think from a choreography standpoint it's
interesting. Because Spider-Man's never fought
[alongside] Spider-Man before, and I think what we
wanted to try to figure out was our individual, unique
styles of how to be Spider-Man.

But I think when you design an action sequence, you
design it around the villain, because they all have their own
different attributes and their different powers, [whereas]
Spider-Man is the same throughout the films. So working
with Ock and working with Goblin and working with
Electro, trying to figure out the different styles so we could
kinda portray those sequences, was so fun. And the amazing
thing about working with Marvel Studios and Sony is that

the sky's the limit with these films. If you want to do a
quadruple backflip over an electric zap or something, that
can happen. It was fun just being able to sit down, play with
the stunt team and figure out how we were gonna make this
film bigger and better than anything before.

What was it like to work with such a great cast?
It's like an actor's dream. The beauty of making these films
is we're so lucky we get to do them with people like Tobey
and Andrew, and people like Marisa Tomei and Jon Favreau
and Willem [Dafoe] and Alfred [Molina] and Jamie [Foxx].
So for me, it means I get to learn from more people. I think
the best way to learn is to watch, and for me to watch the
way they work is amazing. It was a bit of a masterclass for
me, so I couldn't be luckier. ☻

DOCTOR STRANGE

Stephen Strange returns to the Marvel Cinematic Universe in *No Way Home* – but when a memory spell goes wrong, it has unexpected consequences. Benedict Cumberbatch talks about huge sets, Jon Watts's imagination, and slipping on Epsom salts.

How did it feel to be back in the Sanctum?

It's always nice to be back in the Sanctum, and there's nothing like grounding your character in a ridiculously huge set. It felt great to be him again, and it was awesome to be back on the home ground. It's wonderful.

I got to play a little domestic scene or two - this idea that Strange does have a life outside of fighting demons and monsters and gods and who knows what else. That was really good fun to play. But also, it fills you with confidence about being him again, because it's a really extraordinary home to be in. It makes you stand tall. It makes you feel like a bit of a hero.

Can you describe how Strange connects with Peter in the film?

Peter Parker's got a problem with anonymity. He's now world famous, and he wants to go back to a time where the world didn't know him. So he thinks, who better to help time go backwards or forwards than Doctor Strange? Which is a compliment but one riddled with a massive flaw: he doesn't have the Time Stone anymore! Stange still thinks that he can help him, but it goes a little bit wrong when he tries to cast a spell of forgetfulness.

Basically, Peter is someone who wants to become a normal kid again. He can't get into college. He can't be a friend who just goes down the road or goes to a restaurant or a bar or just hangs out at college. Everything's gotten very weird. He's trying to get into college, and he's been denied because there's very mixed feelings about him [with] everybody in the public eye… So he's struggling with all of that and wants to pursue his dream of going to MIT with MJ and Ned. He comes to [Strange] to reverse his predicament, basically – and it all goes horribly wrong!

What makes these characters a great pairing?

They're Super Heroes who are sort of local to one another in New York. Tom and I always joked about it: we said it would be really cool if one of them had a problem, they could just come round to the other's [house] to sort it out! From that, something evolved. And, you know, Tom and I get on very well. We've done a couple of films together other than *Marvel Studios' Avengers: Infinity War* and *Avengers: Endgame*. He and I just get on very well.

And then in the big ballpark of a huge *Avengers* movie, there we stood like, you know, two Brits abroad kinda going, "This is amazing!" Tom's got a lot more experience, actually, than I have of movies at this level. He was just coming off of the success of the first *Spider-Man* film when we were on set [together] for the first time in *Avengers: Infinity War*. And he hasn't looked back, basically. It's been amazing to watch him evolve and swing with it.

It's a pleasure to work with him. He's so inventive. He so knows the character. He knows the world. He knows all the dynamics, all the relationships. And within those parameters, he's constantly reinventing things, coming up with new ideas - brilliant physical pratfalls and stunts as well. You know, he's very gymnastic and athletic. But he's really switched on. It's a happy set, to be on Tom's set.

02

"You know if you're making [Jon Watts] laugh you're halfway to doing something right!"

01 Doctor Strange prepares to cast a spell that will have far-reaching consequences.

02 Wizard vs webslinger as Doctor Strange and Spider-Man grapple on the streets of New York.

03 Doctor Strange casts an elaborate spell.

▶ **Did you have to tackle Tom over maintaining secrecy while you were shooting?**
Well, he was making dinner plans with Alfred Molina. I was like, "No one at this point knows that Doc Ock's in the picture!" So he went, "Oh, yeah, that would be like a paparazzi field day." He is just sort of unfiltered, Tom, which is very, very endearing.

This is the first time you've worked with director Jon Watts, isn't it?
I love Jon. Jon's the bee's knees. He's super smart. He's really sweet. He's incredibly kind and supportive, but he's got a great sense of humor. You know if you're making him laugh, you're halfway there to doing something right! He's just a very affable character with a brilliant imagination. And he was so excited to have this toy of Doctor Strange to play with.

So it felt like you could kind of go anywhere with it, which is what you want in these films. You want to feel that you're kind of free to do new things and discover what the character is like in a very different context and really explore that dynamic with Spider-Man – [you can] see that he and Parker are kind of level in the Avengers. They're two very important Super Heroes, but on the more everyday level, one's in his mid-40s and the other one's yet to go to college. So there's a very paternal or avuncular thing that kind of kicks in with Strange, which is very non-Strange territory to be in! This guy is quite a self-involved egotist, even if he is doing good for others. It's on his own terms. So this kid kind of reorientates him. Jon and I just loved riffing off that and also just doing some really cool stuff that I hadn't done yet as Strange.

14

"It was fun to play on the set. It just puts you right back on your game as a character like Strange."

▶ **Is it helpful to be on a set instead of in front of a green screen?**
Oh, for sure. I mean, that's what Marvel does so well. Obviously, we know that they do the most extraordinary things with VFX. But also, the scale of what they do in live action is not to be underestimated. And the quality of the set build, the paintwork, the effects.

I mean, there was a huge amount of Epsom salts [to create the snow in the Sanctum]. I kid you not! Tons and tons of Epsom salts. When you wet it down, it starts getting that slightly crystallized, squelchy feel of snow that's thawed a little bit after a few hours of sun in the morning. Basically, it's really nice powder, but also a little bit slippy as well. So, you know, we're Super Heroes who are kind of losing our balance!

That's the Jon Watts way, as well. To show people who have super powers going, "Whoops!" and trying not to spill their cups of coffee. So it was fun to play on the set. It just puts you right back on your game as a character like Strange. 😊

05

04 Strange uses his powers to bend reality.

05 This magical relic is used to contain Strange's spell.

ZENDAYA
MJ

Zendaya's fresh take on MJ has been one of the highlights of the Marvel Cinematic Universe *Spider-Man* movies, and *No Way Home* is no exception. The actress talks about how her character has developed over the three films so far and what the role means to her.

Why did you originally want to take on the role of MJ?

It's funny, because when I auditioned I just knew that it was gonna be a *Spider-Man* movie. I didn't really know who the character was. I didn't know the storyline. I didn't know what kind of character she would be. So I was going into it with not much information. But I heard before my chemistry read with Tom that there was a potential "MJ situation" happening.

Now, I've always been a fan of Spider-Man. He's always been my favorite Super Hero. At the end of the day he is just a kid, and has to live this double life. In many ways I can relate to that, having started in the industry so early. Really I'm just a kid. I don't know what I'm doing. I'm just figuring it out as I go, but also simultaneously having this other crazy kind of life. So I've always connected to Peter Parker in that way. And just upon knowing that it was a Spider-Man movie, I knew I wanted to be a part of it. Nobody had to talk me into it!

Once I was cast, [I saw] Jon {Watts}'s vision and his approach to Spider-Man and Peter Parker. The way that he was gonna approach them was so exciting and interesting. His fresh take was just making it feel like real life. What New York feels like, what real students and real people feel like, and turning that into what you see. I felt lucky to be able to be a part of this special journey.

How did MJ's character develop from her first appearance in *Homecoming* to *No Way Home*?

It was fun, because it gave us a bit of a blank slate to work with so we could create this new person. I remember the first conversation that I had with Jon. He explained what her character and her dry humor would be like.

It's been really fun, especially [going] from the first movie being this really guarded, quiet, almost mysterious character that we know nothing about to watching the love story begin between her and Peter at the end of *Far From Home*. And now seeing how being with Peter has really opened her up. She's a very "glass half empty," negative person, but he brings out this hopeful, positive side of her. I think that's really sweet to watch - how they bring out these different parts of each other and rely on each other in different ways.

Do you feel like we see new sides to the character in *No Way Home*?

It's been fun to peel back the different layers of who she is as we've gone through the movies and take our time with her and Peter's relationship... I think what's important is they love each other for who they are. It's clear from the first movie that she's probably loved him long before she figured out that he was Spider-Man. And he appreciates and loves all her quirky takes on life.

What's cool is they each understand each other on a real human level, which allows them to be more vulnerable. That has been the fun thing: watching her become more vulnerable as she knows that Peter loves her. We've been able to chip away at that armor that she's put up her whole life. We have glimpses into MJ's life, and that's reflective of the comics. She has a bit of a tough home life, and I think that that helps her relate to Peter a little more. Understanding the tough things that he has to go through and being there for him.

It's fun to watch MJ and Ned be a part of the action. They get to do as much as they can. They don't have super powers, but they are smart kids. They're doing whatever they can to help the person that they really care about, so sometimes they are in the wrong place at the wrong time. But they're there every step of the way. Peter really needs that support. They rely on each other and I think that's why the friendship works. You need those people in your life, you know?

▶

▶ **Your *Spider-Man* films are a balance of a high school comedy and a huge, intense MCU movie...**
I'm very impressed with how Jon has grown these characters and the stories. I mean, I always love the first movie because it feels like a high school coming-of-age comedy a lot of the time. Like, if I just need to have something to feel cozy and snuggle up to before I get to bed, it has this warmth and this nostalgia to it.

Then it grew even more with *Far From Home*. And this [*No Way Home*] has a whole other level of action. I mean, there's so much going on! We were in awe of what was happening. And the fact that [they] pulled it off - I think that was the craziest part... But I think what's always been important is keeping the heart of the movie, which is Peter. Spider-Man is a big deal, and we all love all the fun and the action that comes with being Spider-Man. But we truly love and care about Peter Parker. That's the one that we want to protect. That's the one that we all tune in to watch because we care about the human story.

How has MJ and Peter's life changed since the world discovered he was Spider-Man at the beginning of this movie?
I remember reading the big reveal in the last movie, and I was like, "No way!" He is who he is because he has this double life. He's able to be a kid and then be a Super Hero, so there's no way we're gonna tell the world who he is. That was such a crazy thought. Then once it

happened, I was like, "Where the hell are we gonna go from here?" The heartbreaking thing, for me, as someone who cares about Peter and MJ, is the fact that they got probably just a few weeks to just enjoy being kids in a new relationship and in love... and then everything explodes in their face. I was like, "No, they deserve happiness!"

But the good thing is that they all really care about each other. They have each other's backs, and Ned has their backs too. They kind of create this safe place with each other because the world feels very crazy. I think Peter just feels so incredibly guilty that anything he touches is affected by his very public life. I can relate to that, I guess, in my own way. Anybody who is around me, their life is connected to me. Like my little nieces, they don't like telling people who their aunt is at school. Anything I do reflects on them, and they feel connected to that: anything good or bad, they probably have to deal with. So I understand not wanting to burden other people with your life.

How do you feel about meeting the other Spider-Men?
I was quite young when the first ones came out, but I remember going to the movie theater and seeing all of them. I've always loved Spider-Man. So when I first heard that this was gonna happen... I mean, this was something that I think all of us on set on the previous movies would have been like, "How cool would it be if this [happened]?" But we knew that that was *never* gonna happen. So when I get in a room with Jon and our producers, and they're

talking about what the movie is gonna be, and how we're gonna have Tobey and his Spider-Man and Andrew and his Spider-Man there... I was like, "How are you gonna do that?" They'd have to put the suit on [again] after all this time, and maybe they don't want to. Maybe they're over it. I couldn't believe it was gonna happen. For all of us that moment of seeing all three Spider-Men together on set was so crazy. It's things that you think about in your head but never believe that you're gonna see in real life.

What added to that was just how lovely everyone was. We all became "FOS" together: Friends of Spider-Man. And now I'm friends with Spider-*Men*. I know all of them! They were so lovely and so thoughtful about their respective Spider-Men because they care about their characters too. They care about their Peters and their different stories. Each of them has a connection to Peter Parker and has this strong relationship because they've lived with those characters for so long.

Did you re-watch the previous *Spider-Man* movies while you were making *No Way Home?*
I saw all the other *Spider-Man* [films] so many times because I just needed to refresh my brain as to who's a villain and who has fought who and why! I would suggest watching all the movies before you see this one just to make sure that you've caught up and you understand what's going on - because it's a lot. There are so many villains and storylines to track!

Can you talk about that pivotal moment when MJ is saved by Andrew Garfield's Spider-Man?
What's interesting is I got to kind of tie up all of these other movies that weren't even mine! I just got to come in and do the fun part. But it was cool because each of these characters has so much pain and trauma from their different experiences as Spider-Man and Peter Parker. So when they meet our Peter Parker they have a huge amount of empathy for what he's going through, because not many people can understand what it's like to be Spider-Man... All of them have made decisions in the past that they regret or has made them compromise who they are as a person. They've had to deal with that darkness or sadness or pain. I just think that they want to make sure he doesn't go through what they went through. They see the relationship that he has with MJ. They see the relationship that he has with Ned. They see what kind of kid he is, and they want to help protect that. So they swoop in almost like big brothers...

So that is a really special scene, and we get to tie up loose ends for other characters. Andrew's Peter Parker gets to help save someone else's love, which is huge for him because it's something he must deal with every single day. When you lose someone that you love and you feel like it was your fault, it is a huge burden to bear, and he's not gotten through it. So when he sees the love that MJ and Peter share, and the fact that there's a moment where he can fix something that he couldn't fix before, it is huge for him, and adds to his healing and his growth. It's a ▶

01 Zendaya returns as MJ.

02 Peter, MJ, and Ned: an inseparable trio,.

03 MJ and Peter enjoy a late night virtual conversation

04

> ## "I think that at the heart of any movie, no matter how big or how small, is the human connections within it."

really sweet moment because MJ doesn't know what happened. She just knows that he just saved her, so she's like, "Thank you!" He's crying, and she's like, "Are you OK?" Even though she's the one that just fell from the building.

Do you think much of the success of the *Spider-Man* movies lies in their relatable characters?
Well, I think at the heart of any movie, no matter how big or how small, is the human connections within it. The things that we as human beings can relate to, which are friendship and love and loss and guilt and all the things that we experience on a day-to-day basis. I mean, we may not have super powers, but we all know what it's like to go through these things. No matter how big a movie can be, it still feels connected to us.

What was it like to work with so many classic villains?
It was so crazy. We go on set and there's Willem Dafoe. And then you see him in his costume - you're like, "Oh my gosh, that's so cool!" Then you see Alfred [Molina] over here and then you see Jamie [Foxx]... It blew my mind every day. And everyone's so sweet and kind and thoughtful and cares about their characters, cares about the other characters, gives so much, and works hard. It's pretty cool that you got all these heavy hitters and iconic performers in one space.

Do you enjoy the wirework on these films?
I love doing that stuff. It's so fun. It's like, "What are you doing at work today?" "Oh, you know, I put a harness on and jumped off this thing." It's so fun because, number one, we have an incredible team of people who make sure that we are safe. And number two, whenever in the world will I be able to experience this stuff? So it's the coolest job ever... And I get to do it with my friends who I've gotten to know and love.

Sony executive and producer Amy Pascal has been involved with the *Spider-Man* films for 20 years. What do you think her legacy will be?
I don't know how she's pulled it off. This is really her baby in a lot of ways because she's seen these movies from the very beginning. She's had these close, personal relationships, not just with the characters but with the people who play the characters. I think they all feel connected to her. I can't imagine how crazy it must feel to see all your Spider-Men together after this many years of being able to be on every single set...

She makes sure that the actors feel like they have a say in what happens to their characters emotionally... She wants to make sure that everyone is happy and a part of the process and feels like their character is being taken care of and their voices are being heard. That's a great quality to have in a producer.

04 Filming a scene that will eventually have the New York cityscape added.

05 Zendaya and Jacob Batalon film on the blue screen set.

What have these films meant to your career?
When I was auditioning for it and doing the first movie, I was just getting started. I mean, it was my first big film. So that was exciting and nerve wracking, and I didn't really know what the future held. I hoped that there would be other movies, but you never really know. And I had this small role in the first one, which I was so grateful for. I was like, "I have no problem saying a couple lines in a Spider-Man movie." I feel lucky to just be in a Spider-Man movie...

But all of us have been able to grow together from the first movie to now. To experience all these incredible changes and beautiful memories together has been very special. I love the people that I get to work with - and that includes not only our beautiful cast but also Jon and all of our incredible producers. I mean, they gave me one of my first shots to do anything other than what I was already doing. That belief in me and my career, I'm forever grateful for. Because that's the belief you need to

be able to try things and go to the next level. They must've seen something, and I appreciate that. That was the seed that continued to help everything grow. And we have our memories documented from the first movie to now...

Even days that I wasn't needed, I came on set to watch because I love learning about the industry and sitting behind Jon. Hopefully one day I'll be able to direct something, and there's no better place to learn than right behind our incredible director!

You've played some very different characters in your career so far.
I think it's important as an actor to be able to experiment. So I can play a grown woman who is my age in some films, and then I can go be a high school student who happens to be with a Super Hero and helps him cure villains from different dimensions! As an actor, all you want is to continue to expand and grow and stretch yourself in a million different ways. ●

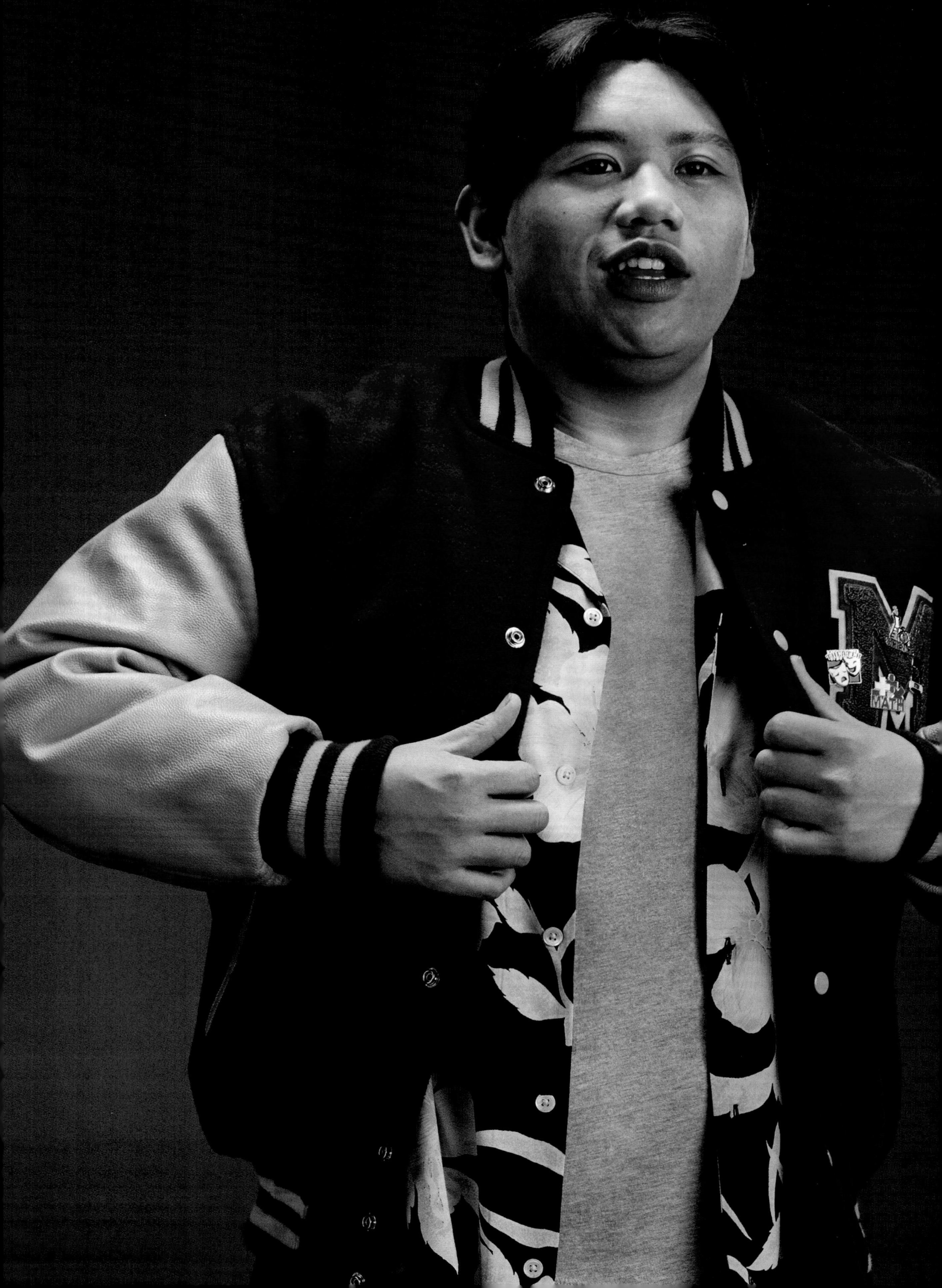

`02`

JACOB BATALON
NED LEEDS

In *Spider-Man: No Way Home*, Jacob Batalon once again reprises his role as Peter Parker's ultra-smart best friend Ned. Here, he looks back on first being cast as Peter Parker's best pal.

What was it like being cast as Spider-Man's best friend?
What was really crazy was that they told me they were going to let me know within two weeks after the audition [for *Spider-Man: Homecoming*]. And I didn't hear from them for like a good two and a half months! When my manager finally called me up about it, it was at, like, 10:47 at night - the oddest time! And he told me that Marvel Studios had chosen to move forward on the option on my contract. He didn't really specify what the role would be. He just said I would be in the movie.

I'm not gonna lie. I was pretty bummed. It wasn't until two weeks prior to me flying in that I finally found out I was Ned. So that whole time waiting, I [thought] I'm probably just gonna be a background guy. I'm probably just going to have two or three lines... And I was in the deepest depression because I was just like, man, they didn't call me up!

Did it feel weird to go back to high school?
Well, back in Hawaii my school is basically two separate buildings. And it's in an open floor plan basically. There wouldn't technically be hallways, and there's a big open space in between the two buildings. The upstairs is a balcony. There's no wall. It's really nice, but it didn't seem like a high school. This [film franchise] gave me the weirdest chills, because I've never been in a high school like this!

How would you describe Ned's character?
He's a very sweet and genuine guy. I think what makes him so genuine is the fact that he loves the whole fact of ignorance is bliss. It doesn't matter what other people do around them. He's just OK being him. And I love that about Ned... And he's a very curious guy. He loves to know things. And the things he has passions for, he can never really let go of them!

You seem to have a natural chemistry with Tom Holland...
People really liked each other from the get-go... I feel like the environment they put us in too was just so friendly and so professional at the same time. There wasn't too much pressure. 😊

01 Jacob Batalon as Ned Leeds.

02 Wielding the power of Doctor Strange's sling ring!

03 The affable Ned finds himself working with Doctor Strange.

04 Batalon and Zendaya shoot a high octane action sequence as MJ and Ned run for their lives!

05 Batalon rehearses a scene with Tom Holland and Zendaya.

06 Ned goes from studying science to using the mystic arts!

03

04

05

06

01

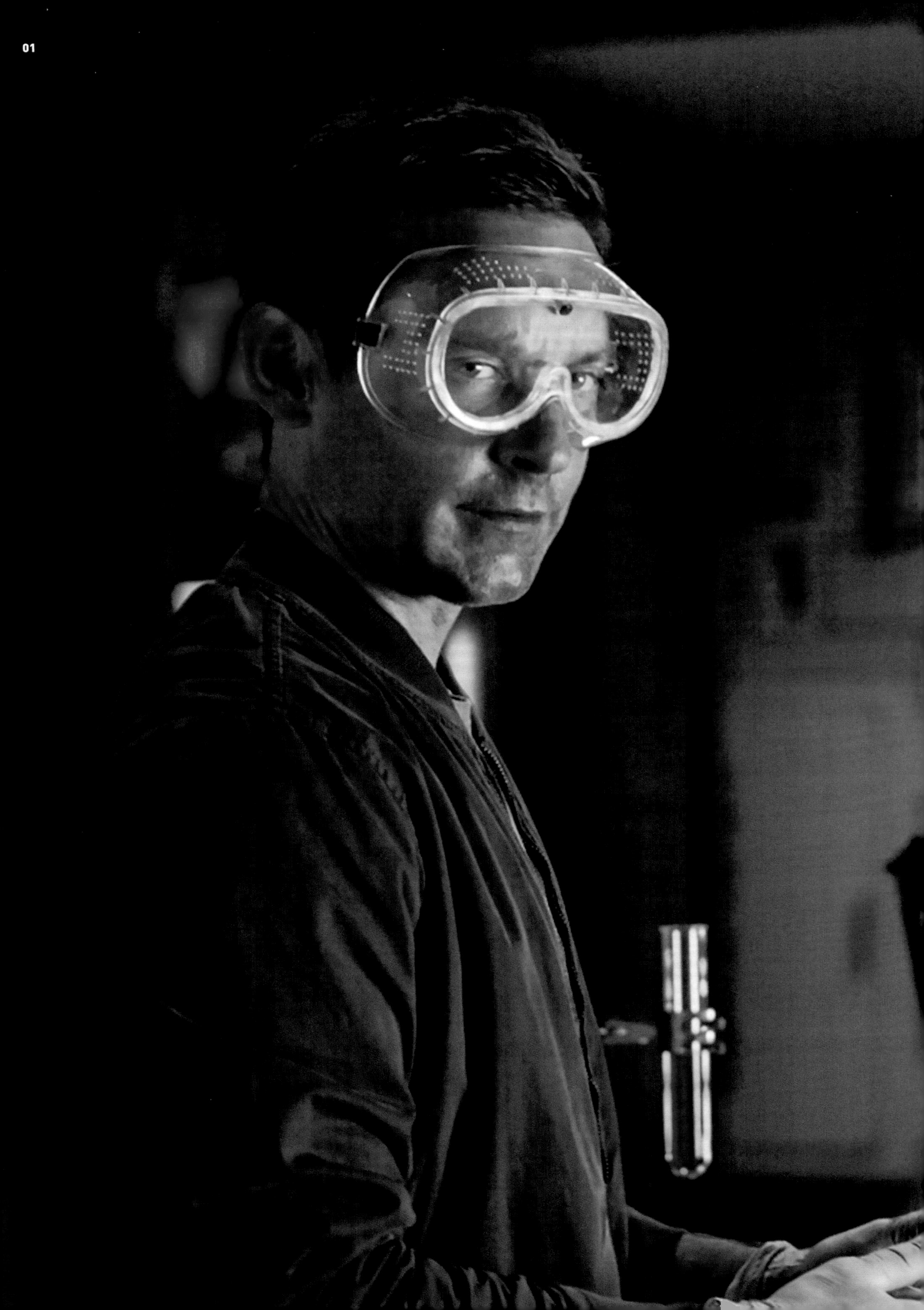

TOBEY MAGUIRE
SPIDER-MAN

When Tobey Maguire first played Spider-Man back in 2002, the Marvel Cinematic Universe didn't even exist. Now his ground-breaking incarnation of the web-slinger is back as part of the multiverse-shattering *Spider-Man: No Way Home*.

The original 2002 *Spider-Man* had a big influence on the Super Hero films that followed…
I want to comment on the history of the genre. For me as a kid, I was watching Super Hero movies. In my experience there are plenty of terrific films and performers who take it seriously. It was maybe more erratic, and it kind of got more cohesive in time.

I've heard people talk about how our Sam Raimi movies were some kind of influential turning point in these movies, which is really sweet and feels like an honor. And not to take away from all the great work that everybody did there, but for me, I have so much love and respect for what came before. I just wanted to acknowledge that!

How did you feel when you got the call about this movie?
When they called initially, I was like *finally*! [Laughs] I got the call and was immediately open about coming to do this. Not without nerves - you know, "What will this look like and what will the experience be?" But to get to show up with beautiful, talented, creative people and play together? It's just like, "Yes!" It's fun and exciting.

I love these films and I love all of the different series. If these guys called me and said, "Would you show up tonight to hang out and goof around?" or "Would you show up to do this movie or read a scene or do a Spider-Man thing?", it would be a "yes!" Because why wouldn't I want to do that?

How did it feel to put on the Spider-Man suit again?
The suit can definitely be a challenge at times when you've got to get in the full thing. But then, once you're comfortable, there is something fun about it. As an actor, it helps when you get in your costume. You begin to feel it more and embody it more… You start to feel pretty at home pretty swiftly.

Did you consider your earlier character arcs when you were working on this film?
I was kind of just in the process for this. It's possible things came to me that felt like a continuation of who this person is, but it [the *Spider-Man* franchise] has evolved in certain ways. I was open to the newness of it and what Tom [Holland] and Jon [Watts] and everyone has done with these movies, which is its own thing. I did have thoughts about how to come in and support and fit into this world, and hold a sort of continuity. But what I realized is that it's almost not necessary, because somehow that history just exists in me.

I had nerves [over] "How do I do this?" and work myself in. And then I just showed up and started talking ▶

02

"I was just like a kid in a candy store feeling energized and perked up and ready to play!"

▶ and that stuff evaporated. There is a falling into it, with the characters and the connectivity, you know? And when Tom and Andrew [Garfield] and Jon and other folks were getting together, the ball started bouncing around and I was just having fun and not thinking about those [earlier] movies.

No Way Home boasts a great cast – some of whom you had worked with on your earlier *Spider-Man* movies...
On my first day going up to the set and just saying hi to folks, out walks Alfred Molina and out walks Marisa Tomei, Willem Dafoe, Tom, and Jamie [Foxx]. We're all just standing in this little area. And I'm coming from being at home social distancing in Los Angeles for the last ten months! We all had masks on, but I was there in this exciting circle of people that just brought me joy, both from certain personal memories or connections and also from what they've given as artists. I was just like a

kid in a candy store feeling energized and perked up and ready to play!

Are you surprised by the evolution of the *Spider-Man* franchise over the years?
I am pretty amazed with the evolution in time and the connectivity through the Marvel Cinematic Universe. And then how you know whether [a film is] in the MCU or not... this sort of conversation that all these movies are having with each other, where one movie does whatever it does and then that informs the next thing.

It's fun to watch it unfold and continue to evolve and find the unique little paths that these different movies take... It's really sophisticated and interesting and it just keeps unfurling. Then you think, "It's gotten as good as it can get" and it's just like, "Boom!" - some next step breaks ground and opens up a bunch of new possibilities. It's been fun to watch over the years, just as a fan. ☻

01 Peter Parker shows off his science skills.

02 Joining the battle against the villains, including the vengeful Green Goblin.

03 Maguire did not take the chance to return to the role of Spider-Man lightly.

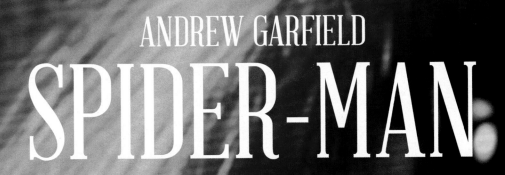

ANDREW GARFIELD
SPIDER-MAN

Back in 2012, *The Amazing Spider-Man* saw Andrew Garfield don the costume in an energetic reboot, which was followed by a sequel in 2014. The actor thought he was finished with the role – until he heard the wild pitch for *No Way Home*. He opens up about auditioning, working with his fellow Spider-Men, and what it's *really* like to wear the Spider-Man suit.

Were you always a Spider-Man fan?
It was my first Halloween costume when I was two or three. My mom made this felt, hand-sewn, adorable, baggy Spider-Man outfit. Since then, it's been my favorite Super Hero, I suppose.

I was a huge fan of Tobey's movies. I actually re-watched his second movie the other night, and it holds up beautifully. The essence of that character comes through so beautifully, and he's such a remarkably good fit. I was conflicted when I heard that they were gonna do another [Spider-Man film after *Spider-Man 3*], because [Maguire's take on the character] is so seminal. This was before I even thought I would be auditioning for it. But also, I thought, "It makes sense because the character is so important to so many people. It can be anyone in that suit, and they'll just reinvent it in a new way. And I will pay money to see that character in any film!"

How was your original audition?
When I got a chance to audition, I thought, "How cool would it be to fulfill some weird version of a childhood dream?" So, of course, I auditioned and didn't really think much of it in terms of [if] I would get it or not. Then they asked me to do a screen test, and I suddenly thought, "This could happen. This could be a thing that will change my life." Obviously, that created conflict in the sense of, "Do I want to be that recognizable? Do I want to take on this responsibility?" But then, of course, I did want to! So I decided to screen test and throw my hat in the ring.

I was really nervous at that point, because I was like, "I really would like to do this!" And when you want to do something and may not get to do it, then suddenly everything becomes very intense. You have to just take big risks and leave it to the gods.

Because I was so nervous and wanted it so much, I figured out a way of doing the screen test. I gave myself an acting adjustment, I suppose, which was: you're a 15-year-old and you're making a *Spider-Man* short film with mates. All the crew are friends. There's no pressure. You get to make it up as you go along, and it's about the joy of being this character. I was able to trick my ego to be occupied in a corner. I convinced the part of me that puts pressure on myself that it wasn't needed and that we were just gonna go and have a laugh. I think that meant I was able to show up fully and be really present and have a good time. I worked hard at it, but then it was just about throwing it away and seeing what happened.

What was your initial approach to the character?
For me, the essence of Spider-Man and Peter Parker is constant, no matter who plays the character or whatever incarnation of the comics. There are certain essential qualities of Peter Parker and Spider-Man that are immovable and sacrosanct. The essence of ultimate goodness. Being a servant to humanity and to all living things. Being an underdog, someone who sticks up for the have-not's, someone who is an everyman, a kind of

02

"Tom Holland has all the pressure and we get to help him and support him as big brothers!"

working-class hero. Someone who struggles with their ordinariness in conflict with their extraordinariness… Someone who struggles with, I suppose, [the fact] of "With great power comes great responsibility." Those things are immovable.

That's great, because then you have this incredible foundation of goodness that you get to build upon. I think each incarnation of the character has to struggle with what being good means. But for me, where I deviated… it's tough for me to talk about that, because I try not to be too aware of those things. I just try and follow my instinct. But it was a moment in time where the "high school nerd" was taking over the world and was becoming, for better or worse, kind of our culture. So, for me, it was like, "Well, Tobey's brilliant nerdiness, which made him an underdog, doesn't really work anymore for the particular cultural moment that we're in." So it was like, so how do we make him an underdog? How do we make him an outsider?

For me, that was about his being an orphan and honing in on the emotional turmoil of lacking a

01 The Amazing Spider-Man (Andrew Garfield).

02 Spider-Men unite on the Statue of Liberty.

connection to an identity... Not that all orphans lack identity, but I think this particular orphan, my Peter Parker, was searching for connection to something that he could feel but didn't quite understand. There was a longing to know if he was abandoned, whether he was lovable... He's a brilliant scientist and mathematician, but doesn't trust people entirely because of that fear of abandonment. That was my approach.

How did it feel to get the call about *No Way Home*?
It was a shocking call to receive, because I had thought I had put it to bed and said, "Thank you, I'm gonna go this way." This was a really important formative period of my life: I got to play that part, and I got to meet the people that I worked with, and we had all the multitude of experiences that we'd had. It was a really beautiful and educational part of my life. I can't deny there was always something that was in the back of my head - like, "Gosh, it ended a bit abruptly for me." But I had made peace with that. And, of course, just like when you break up with someone and you've started to finally move on, they always know when to call!

That's kind of what occurred - where I was like, "I've let that experience go, and I'm very happy with how it went..." - and then I got the call, and it's Amy [Pascal] going, "We got a great idea...." Amy organized a call with Kevin [Feige] and the absolutely brilliant director, Jon Watts, to talk me through what they were thinking. We did a Zoom, and I was kinda like, "Oh, that sounds great."

The Marvel Studios pedigree is what it is. There is a certain amount of assurance that you have as an actor coming in going, "Well, I don't think it's possible for them to mess this up because they do what they do." And Kevin is such a fanboy himself of these characters and stories that you feel like he's the ultimate audience for these films, shaping them. So you go with him as a safety net. And with Amy, who has been with this character for 20 years, there's real care and artistry and support there.

Then I met Jon. I loved what he did with these [earlier *Spider-Man*] movies, where you go, "Oh, this could be a great thing to be involved with" and not have [to carry] all of the pressure for the first time on one of these sets. I think for me and Tobey, this was really fun. A lot of that is to do with [the fact that] Tom Holland has all the pressure, and we get to help him and support him as big brothers. He's carrying it, so we get to just be of service to him and of service to the film. So they pitched me the idea, and I was like, "I want to see that on screen." I listened as a fan first. It resulted in this very beautiful experience where I got to have a bit more closure on something that means so much to me.

How would you describe your emotional arc in the film?
Just showing up and doing a cute cameo would've been a cool moment for an audience and for me. But adding some depth and healing to this invisible character arc that's been happening for the last however-many years in my Peter Parker's dimension...There's something so profound about it thematically, which is this idea that all human life, in this dimension or any other dimension, is interconnected. And [there's] another theme, which I think is great: that our deepest wounds are our greatest ▶

gifts. The fact that I'm coming into this dimension as Peter Parker with this terrible gaping wound that I haven't yet healed, and that I get to dive back into that wound for the sake of my little brother - so it becomes a healing moment... There's something profoundly beautiful in that.

How did you find working with your fellow Spider-Men, Tom Holland and Tobey Maguire?
I think myself, Tom, and Tobey came into this going, "Well, how's this gonna go?" I'd had lovely interactions with Tom and Tobey previously; not big hangouts, but really sweet moments at parties or events - or as sweet and as deep as those things can go, which is not very! But I got a really good vibe from Tom and a really good vibe from Tobey. So I was excited to get to know these guys more and to see what we could create together.

We all came with our own history and with our own relationship to the character in our own films. I think what really was wonderful, and how it unfolded very early on, was Tobey and I felt very aligned and very clear about what our intentions were for being there. Ultimately, it was to serve Tom as an actor and, as characters, serving Tom's Peter Parker. I think from that place, everything flowed. It enabled Tobey and me to have a bit more fun maybe than we would've had if we were the ones fully carrying the story.

How did you find working with Jon Watts?
It was Jon that really started to excite me about the creative possibilities... I'm in awe of what Jon Watts did here. Because he carries the weight of the film so lightly, but he's not afraid of going deep. He's not afraid of going crazy and weird and [using] offbeat humor when that's called for. And he's able to keep a light, fun set while having all this responsibility. I'm a big admirer.

The great thing about Jon is that he's like, "OK, here are the sides for today. Let's read it out loud, and we'll see what works and what doesn't. And what doesn't work, we'll just make it up, and we'll do it until it feels right and until it feels real and the best possible version of this scene." That's kind of what we did every day. And when you get a bunch of talented people putting their hearts and minds into something they care about, and when it's "best idea wins" and no one has ownership over the ideas, suddenly you can go anywhere.... It feels like Jon was trying to make an indie film on a budget this size.

The film has a great cast of villains from the previous films – including Jamie Foxx reprising the role of Electro...
It's pretty cool. I've never worked with Alfred or with Willem, so I was really excited about that. And it's impossible not to have a good time with Jamie. He's so inventive. He's so creative. He had the crew laughing

03

on the Sony lot. And I'm no spring chicken anymore. That was something that I wanted to bring into the dynamic between the Peters - you know, leaning into the slightly "creaky back, creaky bones, less-easy-to-hold-the-poses" version of the character.

Were you conscious of the impact that seeing three incarnations of Spider-Man on-screen would have on audiences?
In shooting this I had no concept of that objective thing of [seeing] three Spider-Men in the same frame on screen. I had no awareness of the impact of that. It's not my job to, in a way. Me, Tom and Tobey – we were just like, "How do we do our job?" - which is to make it real, entertaining, emotional, joyful, and make a real dynamic between the three of us.

There was a moment when we were shooting that scene [where the three Spider-Men are together in frame for the first time]. When we finished the first take, Tom and I looked at each other. Tom was like, "Something doesn't feel right." And I was like, "I know, we haven't figured out what this is yet. It feels like we're missing something." Straight after that moment, Jon comes up the scaffolding, and he's like, "It's great. It's amazing. Go again." Tom and I look at each other, and we're like, "We have no idea what's going on in the monitors!" So we did a few more takes, and we tried to figure out what we were doing. We were just unaware of what they were seeing down there! But we kinda figured out what the scene was for us and we felt better about it. Then we went down, and Jon was like, "Come and look at the playback." And it's just the image of Tobey, myself, and Tom in our Spider-Man suits filmed from a TechnoCrane, with a bit of a swoop... It was just that iconic image. And I think I understood there that this was gonna be deeply special for people.

As a fan, that's the point in a way. And that image is a unifying one, because everyone has their favorite Spider-Man. Everyone has their favorite actor who has played it or incarnation in the comics. Of course, there's kids fighting at the dinner table about which one [is their favorite] and what should and shouldn't have happened. But that image just kind of dissolves all of that. It goes back to that theme of the interconnectedness of all things: one can't exist without the other. And the lineage... like, I don't exist without Tobey. And Tom doesn't exist without Tobey and me. And we don't exist without Tom! It's a weird thing where we're all part of the same kind of ancestral family.

What has this experience meant to you?
I mean, I've lived a full life since finishing my [earlier] movies creatively and personally, and I'm very grateful for all of it. This is just a piece of beautiful icing on a cake. I feel like, "How did I get so lucky that not only did I get to play the character, but I got to come back and do some healing for the character *and* support another actor playing the character *and* get to be with my childhood favorite playing that character?" I don't take it lightly. 🕷

constantly. He's a great storyteller and the complete character. We both love improvising, so we just got there on the day and felt out what the moment was. We kept it loose, kept it spontaneous, and it was really fun. And it was really awesome to watch Willem and Alfred work as well, because I'm such a big admirer of their careers. It's a crazily special group of people.

Do you have a favorite villain from the movies?
For me, Alfred as Doc Ock... the humanity that he brought to that character and the darkness that he brought felt so real. I kind of can't understand how he did it! Re-watching the second *Spider-Man* recently, the way that he moves and the way that those tentacles operate is so brilliant. It's so smart, and so simple how the machine takes over and he has to use all of his will at the end to be the master of the machine. Then that moment where the tentacles kowtow to him... It's absolutely brilliant creative design.

And Willem's Goblin being so comic book-y and grotesque, and the contrast between his Norman and his Goblin... It shouldn't work, but it works so brilliantly. It's genuinely scary and camp. Willem is just fearless. He's so unselfconscious as an actor, just totally free.

How did it feel to don the Spidey suit again?
Same suit! They pulled it out of some dusty storage unit

03 Spider-Men from across the Multiverse join forces.

WILLEM DAFOE
GREEN GOBLIN

Willem Dafoe was unforgettable in the role of disturbed businessman Norman Osborn and his malevolent alter ego the Green Goblin in 2002's *Spider-Man* and its two sequels. The actor was excited to return to the role for *Spider-Man: No Way Home*.

How did you feel about returning to the franchise?

You know when I heard it I thought, "Well that's pretty nutty!" I got speared pretty good in the first film. I thought, "OK, they can figure out a way to bring me back…"

Jon [Watts], the director, kind of pitched the whole idea before I read a script, and it sounded like a lot of fun and a good solution [to the fact that the Green Goblin was dead]. Then when we went deeper into it, I liked the idea that I was returning to something that was the same but different. I mean, it's a return to something I did before with that kind of history, but there's a [new] spin on it, and that appwealed to me.

How did you find getting back into the Green Goblin costume?

You want to know the truth? Nobody knows how uncomfortable those costumes are! But they look good. We are actors - you forget about the discomfort and, you know, it's part of it. But the costumes are much more comfortable than they were before. I remember the initial fitting to create the costume for the Green Goblin [for the 2002 movie]. I stood there for eight hours and they put different pre-formed pieces on me. Now they scan me, they design it, then they make the costume, and *then* they try it on me. It's a huge leap in the technology and [the costumes] are more flexible. We can do more things with them.

Also, the look's a little different. Old Norman and the Goblin are further down the line and they have a few more tricks up their sleeve. So there were upgrades on the costume, which was cool.

Do you enjoy playing the two sides of the character?
To me that was one of the beauties of it. That really rooted the villain character, because the [Green Goblin] character basically was a look and action [sequences] and wisecracks and stuff like that, but really what rooted you being with that character was Norman Osborn, who is sort of a tragic figure. [That was] something I could get behind.

Did you enjoy working with the other actors reprising villainous roles, such as Alfred Molina and Jamie Foxx?
The nice thing is when you have people that want to be there, and this isn't their first rodeo, it's a real good working situation. And flexibility and generosity are two of the qualities that you want in an actor, and these guys are like that.

How did you find working with Tom Holland?
Tom Holland is crazy good! He's really impressive, and also physically he's just very agile and really skilled in doing the stunt stuff and the fighting stuff. He's a freak, man, he's really good.

Like your original Spider-Man films, this movie boasts some spectacular visual effects…
Because this franchise has been so successful clearly they have the resources to do really adventurous and really sophisticated things. Not only in effects, for example, [but] the sets… It's very high level!

Were you surprised to be embarking on the Spider-Man journey again?
Yes, yes, yes! [Laughs] ☻

01 The Green Goblin returns to menace not just one but three Spider-Men!

02 Peter Parker confronts the Green Goblin.

03 Norman Osborn shows off some of the Goblin's deadliest upgrades.

04 Osborn goes incognito as he adapts to the new universe.

ALFRED MOLINA
DOC OCK

For many fans, Alfred Molina's Doc Ock in *Spider-Man 2* is the greatest villain of any of the films in the franchise. The actor talks about how it felt to return to the Spider-verse and reveals how he got back into character.

Did you ever think you would return to the role of Doc Ock?

I didn't think that [Doc Ock] was ever gonna come back because in Sam Raimi's *Spider-Man 2*, he died! But I remember on the day I wrapped, I said to Avi Arad, who was one of the producers on that movie, "Well, I guess you won't be using the option you had seeing as I'm dead!" Because contractually they had an option on me for another movie. And he said, "Well, in this universe nobody dies..." I kind of thought he was just being a joker, because in the comics the characters come and go. So I kinda laughed.

But then I was very proud of that film. I'd never done a big tentpole movie, and I was thrilled to be part of it. But I thought that was it. So then I went off and did my little plays and little films here and there. And as the

02

years went by, I did begin to realize just how popular the character was. Not because of anything I did with it, but just in terms of fans of the comic books and fans of the whole genre, he was a very popular character. But I still didn't imagine… I wasn't sitting there thinking, "Oh, one of these days I'm gonna come back!"

When [producer] Amy Pascal got in touch with me about doing it this time, 17 years had gone by. And I suddenly thought, "There's no way." I mean, how's that gonna work? It felt great to be doing it again, but this time I did feel a bigger sense of responsibility because I knew how popular the character is. Whereas before I was loving it in just a very enthusiastic way, this time I was thinking, "I don't want to let the fans down."

Fans were hugely excited when they learnt that Doc Ock was returning.
I think a lot of it was less to do with me and more to do with the way the character was written; the fact that the character had this very well developed backstory [in *Spider-Man 2*]. There's that wonderful scene when he invites Peter Parker to tea, and he's there with his wife. They're holding hands, and they're talking about poetry. They're talking about their life, and they're sharing something with this young student. I remember thinking when I read that scene, "So far, he's this great husband, a successful, brilliant scientist, a great teacher. How are they going to turn him into a bad guy?" And, of course, the Marvel world weaves its magic. A lesser script

wouldn't have had that scene. He would've just been, "Boom! Bad guy." That wouldn't have had anywhere near have the same impact.

All the villains have this wonderful backstory, so you're rooting for these guys. And when the terrible thing happens to them that turns them into villains, I think there's a part of the audience that really cares for them and feels bad for them… Many of them become villains almost reluctantly. An accident or some terrible tragedy happens and it transforms them. That's what makes them very playable. It's not just mustache-twirling. It's got real depth.

Did you feel any sense of pressure about Doc Ock's return?
No, not pressure. I felt responsibility to get it right, certainly. To do as well as I could. But that's a good feeling. I didn't feel, "Oh, god, if I don't get this right, everything's gonna turn to mush." But if this is one of the characters that they're looking forward to seeing again, that's fantastic. I'm honored by that.

In the intervening years since the last one, I've been stopped in the street occasionally, and people say, "Oh, I loved you in *Spider-Man*." And it never bothers me. It's never an intrusion. I think, "How lucky are we that we've done something that has had such meaning in someone's life?"

How did you get back into character after all those years?
I did go back and look at the first one [*Spider-Man 2*], just to kinda get a sense of the film grammar, if you like. And I wanted to remember some little details, which I'd forgotten. Basically Doc Ock picks up where he left off. So Avi was absolutely right. Nobody dies in this universe!

But I wanted to be able to hit the road running… I wanted to make sure that I was in the right place in terms of the performance. So it was useful to go back and look at the first film, but at the same time it's a different director, it's a different movie, there's a freshness to it. I didn't want to just come back and replicate what we'd done before. It was important to me to arrive as if this was the first time.

How do you think Tom Holland's take on Spider-Man differed from Tobey Maguire's?
Tom is incredibly agile. He's a dancer. He's been a gymnast. He's got this incredible physicality that's both very strong and very rooted. But it's also very elegant because of his dance experience. There's a kind of poetry about the way he moves. There's a language to it, which is very rather beautiful. And I think Tobey's approach was a bit more cerebral. That may be as much to do with them as actors, how they attack things. Because however much we try to be different, with every part we play, we're always bringing ourselves to it.

I looked at all the *Spider-Man* films while I was prepping. And all three of them, Tobey and Andrew and Tom, have got very different qualities and different approaches. I think that's part of what makes the franchise so popular. There was a time, even within my professional lifetime, that the idea of a different actor playing such an iconic role ▶

01 Peter Parker comes face to face with Doc Ock.

▶ would've been thought of as box office death… But if the iconic character is strong enough and fascinating enough, and if the context that you're telling the story in is good enough, then audiences will take it.

How did you find working with Tom Holland?
He's got what I like to call a film intelligence. He understands the angles, he understands the lenses, he understands how you work with the camera to tell the story. I predict within the next five, six years, he's gonna be directing.

There seems to be a real chemistry between you and the actors playing your fellow villains.
I think that there's a mutual respect there. We all know each other's work and we've all been around for a while. There is a sense of camaraderie that comes from a shared experience in terms of, you know, that we've all done one of these before. In Willem's case, more than one. There's a sense that we've arrived at a place where we can enjoy this without being too precious about it. We can enjoy it for all the marvelous things that it's giving us, but also for the absurdities of it - you know, three grown men in these costumes, giving as much energy to it as we would if we were playing Shakespeare!

Did it feel like you were in a theater company of actors?
I think Willem made the point that there's a sense of it being a kind of ensemble because we're sharing the world. And we developed a lot of the scenes as we were shooting them. Jon would have an idea or say, "That was great, but try this." He might even give us an extra bit of dialogue, just to enhance something he wanted to discover in the scene. There was that sense of building the film as we were in the moment. And the emotional range that these characters have – that's meat and potatoes to an actor.

So it was a bit like working in a company, but it wasn't like theater. It's a very different discipline. But the atmosphere and the collegiality, if you like, of the moment was very much like working within a company.

There's a great scene in the Sanctum where you and your fellow villains discuss whether or not you all died.
It was a very interesting scene to work on. But I couldn't help thinking while I was standing in my little portion, "I've got Jamie Foxx over here, I've got Lizard and Sandman over there, I've got Benedict here and Tom's there…. This is so incredibly cool." And I said to Benedict, "This is blowing my mind!"

It constantly did that. I mean, there was a moment all three Spideys and me and Jamie were chatting off-camera while we were waiting to start work. They were in their Spidey suits, I was in my costume, Jamie was in his. We were chit-chatting about, "Oh, so where are staying? When did you get here?" Just little stuff. Suddenly we all went very quiet. And I think we were all doing the same thing. We were just taking this moment in - this extraordinary, unique moment, which probably will never happen again.

02 Universes collide as Doc Ock battles an unexpected Spider-Man!

How did you find the Doc Ock costume this time?
The costume is essentially the same. But the only difference is that because the tentacles weren't attached to me, it gave me a bit more freedom physically. But it meant that whatever we were doing, I had to be aware of them because they were gonna be put in in post. There was a moment on the set where I was standing in a doorway, and my first thought wasn't, "Where's my light?" My first thought was, "Is there room for the tentacles?" And then Jon kinda put me a step beyond the doorway in order to allow that room, because the CG team would be going, "Well, I got nowhere to put it!"

So it gave me a bit more freedom, but in a weird sort of way I missed them being attached. Because when I had them on, each tentacle had two puppeteers operating it. There was sometimes six and sometimes eight people, depending on the shot. Hence, we created what I called the *optorage*, which was this kind of gang of people. They were actors as well; we were kinda working like a little ensemble company. And when we had medium shots and close-ups where you could see a tentacle in

the background, they were working it. If you look at that movie, you'll notice that the tentacles are never still. They're always undulating or reacting. I kinda missed that, but that's all there [in *No Way Home*], just in post.

How do you find working on these big movies where so much is enhanced by CGI later on?
One thing I learnt very quickly the first time I did Doc Ock was that you have to embrace the fact that you are the actor is a small cog in a much bigger machine. Whatever you're doing in front of the camera, in the finished product there's gonna be 101 other things going on behind you or around you that you may not be aware of right now. So you have to bear in mind not just what you're making but how it's being made.

That's why these movies take so long to make. You're making a huge mosaic, but it's one tiny little tile at a time. That's why each moment has to be treated so meticulously to get it absolutely right. The trick is to sustain the same level of intensity and energy each time so you make sure that all the little pieces match. I mean, the thing about working in

front of blue screen is that I find myself relying very heavily on what the director tells me. Because I'll lose perspective about where we're at. I don't know what it's gonna look like. I've got an idea, say, that the New York skyline and the Statue of Liberty is gonna be around me. But in terms of doing it in that moment, I'm sort of all at sea. So I had to rely very closely on what Jon asked me to do, and I wanted to make sure I did exactly what he wanted.

How would you describe Jon Watts's approach as a director?
He's very enthusiastic. He loves this genre. He loves this world. He treats it with respect. He's a fan. But also he loves bringing out the humor. He wants the audience to find it not just dramatic and exciting, but he also wants them to find it as delicious as he does. He wants them to enjoy the moment.

He encouraged us to improvise and to throw in [our ideas]. When he'd got the take that he wanted, he'd always say, "OK, one more to do what you want to do." Some actors, like Jamie, are a master at improv. His brain works so fast. Tom as well. Because Tom's got the experience of playing the character so many times, he just knows the right tone. Me, I'm a terrible improviser! I know my lines, but don't ask me to do something else because I don't have that brain. I just look keen and move with it, but that's not particularly my skill. But [Watts] allowed that freedom.

The other thing, which is really important, is that he takes the work very seriously but not himself. He arrives with an enthusiasm, like he's just come back from the store and he's got a whole bunch of new comics. The fact that he looks about 15 years old doesn't hurt either!

What were you most excited to see in the final movie?
What's really exciting about seeing it with what I call a "proper audience," as opposed to everyone with a vested interest, is listening to the reaction - just being in that space with all those people, and hearing how they respond to it. That's the most gratifying thing. What makes these movies so rewarding is that you're playing to a partisan audience, in a sense. The audience that comes to this movie wants it to be fantastic, and they'll give you some leeway. It's a bit like the uncle that comes to sports day. He's the one that's cheering, "Go on! Yeah!"

But I find it hard watching myself, to be honest. I never watch playback after we've shot a scene. Most actors I've worked with love to go and check it out and, certainly, if there's technical stuff to be concerned with... But I can't do it. I can't watch the playback, because all I see is mistakes. Which is why at the end of each take, I just turn to Jon and go, "Happy?" And he'll either say yes or no. That's all I need to know.

Would you play Doc Ock again?
Who knows? I mean, I'd be up for it. I remember being asked in an interview years ago after *Spider-Man 2* came out, "Would you play the part again?" And I said, "Yes, of course." If you're asking me again, I'd say, "Yes, of course!" It's not just a great part, but it's a real honor to be involved with this. ◉

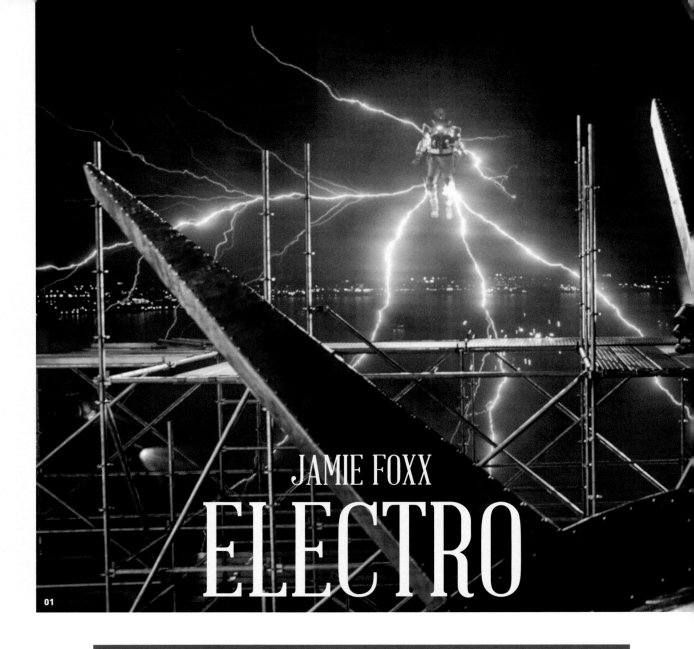

01

JAMIE FOXX
ELECTRO

Spider-Man: No Way Home sees Jamie Foxx reprise his role as the electricity-channeling Electro from *The Amazing Spider-Man 2* – but this time the villain has a very different look.

What was your first reaction on being called back to the franchise?
I was excited. I'd known Amy [Pascal, producer] for years, and knew what she's doing with this franchise... She was explaining to me: it was going to be hot, I didn't have to be blue. Things like that as far as my character's concerned. And I got a chance to hang out with incredible thespians.

How did you find the new Electro costume?
I'm happy we got a brand new start. A brand new look. When I was blue they still rolled with me, but [they were like], "Oh OK, you're *blue*." [LAUGHS]

With this one, it just feels more comfortable. I think it feels more modern, not trying so hard. I sort of relate it to R&B back in the day. You used to have fringes on your outfit and shoulder pads and things like that, but now you can just sing, you know? So now we're just singing.

How did you find working with Tom Holland?
When we first got on the set I said, "Look at this dude's eyes!" And at one point you'll see it - he's trying to figure things out, that's what makes it amazing. Because basically he's torn. He wants to be cool with these [villains], but at the same time they really want to

Why do you think Marvel Studios movies like *No Way Home* are so successful?
I think the beauty of these franchises is the fact that you have such talented actors. The reason being is because if you just rely on the suit, if you just rely on the visual effects, you're in troubled waters. It's the quiet moments [where] you've got to talk about something that happens in the movie, where [a character] does his thing… That's when we, as actors, are like, "This [actor is] incredible. "

They've been fortunate - whether they knew it or not - to have real actors anchor these characters. You can go anywhere with them and feel comfortable asking them to do something. You may need something dramatic in one moment and then, turn on a dime, you're doing something funny. So I think that's why these franchises are so successful.

And I mean guys like Jon [Watts], everybody [else]… We got a lot of great minds here, man. When you have that type of dynamite, that kind of TNT, I mean people are going to go along for the ride… I think [audiences] marvel at not only how they put it together but how they stay *current*, you know what I'm saying? Staying current is a big thing. Like my daughter, who is 12 and who's followed this franchise since she was four - you need something that they understand.

Was your daughter excited to see *No Way Home*?
My daughter had a chance to watch things firsthand. She was on the set, she actually had her face painted blue, and things like that. So she was able to watch the evolution of it and actually understand it. And then their social media networks - they say, "Oh, this is what's happening." They're very smart in how they pay attention to every detail.

It's like the kid in all of us as we continue to grow. It's amazing how [the Marvel Studios movies] continue to keep up with us, and at the same time, bring in children like my daughter's age. Because kids now grasp a billion times more things than we do. Sometimes people would try to play down to kids [with movies], and then lose them. With this, it brings them up, gives them the chance to stretch and really understand the workings of it.

Why do you think Electro is such a great villain?
With Electro, it's the world that did him wrong. You can go all the way back to Shakespeare, when something is personal or it's a jealousy thing. Nothing can beat that - no matter what costume you put on. 🕷

eliminate him… [Tom Holland] anchors it in such a way, that you go like, "Man, I believe this dude is meant to play [this role!]"

And then here's the thing: you're filling big shoes. You know, because we grew up with Tobey. Man, when Tobey hit that wall the first time… and then here comes this young guy with this fresh face and who is really in tune in every aspect. Even when he's not doing anything, he's making sure every character has an angle. He and Jon work so well together. And that freakin' hair! The Spider-Man hair. I was like, "This hair is great!"

You star alongside Willem Dafoe and Alfred Molina, who play other villains from the earlier *Spider-Man* movies. Did you enjoy working with them?
Listen, I'd work with these actors on any project… When people really have the talent, they don't need the extra stuff. When you walk in and you see these guys, oh man… you could spend three or four months of your life in finding these incredible gems on and off camera. Whatever they would like to do, just let me stand somewhere!

01 Sparks fly as Electro makes his presence felt.

> "I'm happy we got a brand-new start, a brand-new look…I was happy to be in this wonderful franchise."

SANDMAN & THE LIZARD

Spider-Man: No Way Home also features returning villains Flint Marko/ Sandman, and Dr. Curt Connors/the Lizard, played once again by Thomas Haden Church and Rhys Ifans, respectively.

01 Sandman looms large over Spider-Man.

02 Electro, Sandman, and the Lizard prepare for battle at the Statue of Liberty.

03 The Lizard is the alter ego of Dr. Curt Connors.

04 The Lizard grapples with his nemesis.

MARISA TOMEI

MAY PARKER

Peter Parker's beloved aunt, May Parker, as played by Marisa Tomei, is a formative figure in Peter Parker's life, even as he faces his greatest challenge in *Spider-Man: No Way Home*.

01

01 With the world now aware of Peter's secret identity, May tries to help her nephew deal with his unwanted celebrity status.

02 May has been a constant inspiration for Peter throughout his adventures.

JON FAVREAU
HAPPY HOGAN

Actor and filmmaker Jon Favreau has played Happy Hogan since 2008's *Marvel Studios Iron Man*. Formerly a close associate of Tony Stark, the character is now on hand to help Peter Parker. Favreau looks back on his 15 years in the Marvel Cinematic Universe.

Does playing Happy Hogan today feel any different than when you first portrayed him in *Iron Man*?
I've sort of gotten past the oddness of what it feels like to be on a Marvel Studios set. The first few were strange, but I have to say now when I come in, it feels very familiar. I know a lot of the crew members, the cast. And when I come in, I really trust a lot because I, like everybody else, don't really get to look at the script until right beforehand - and then it's only the stuff I'm involved with!

Happy Hogan is a really cool character to play because he kind of weaves through things, and I get to be involved with all the emotional moments that connect the films. I love the idea that kids have grown up with these movies and that I help connect it to the movies they saw when they were little.

Did you ever imagine when you directed and appeared in *Iron Man* that the MCU would still be going strong 15 years later?
It is amazing that these little decisions have turned into things that have had ramifications years downstream... I feel like we were doing a lot of discovery on the first one. There was a lot of uncertainty. But we had a really good group of people, and a lot of them are still working on these films. And, of course, [we had] a great cast and great source material. We found a way to put it together with a certain tone, a certain personality, a certain sensibility that they've been able to carry forth and build upon in a way that it

expanded it way beyond anything we ever did.

So, on the one hand, it feels like it is a continuation of what we did. But I'm also always really surprised and delighted by all the new innovations and the new voices, the new characters they're able to bring in, and how much they're able to deviate from what we did in *Iron Man* and still have it feel like one shared universe.

No Way Home shows that Marvel Studios doesn't have an aversion to risk, doesn't it?
Yeah, they're pretty bold at Marvel Studios! I think they're more scared of being complacent than taking chances... So now here we are [with *No Way Home*], and what an interesting take! I really give a lot of credit to Tom for being the host of the party and being inviting and gracious to make room for everyone to be a star. He's a special guy, and it's a special project because of that. Not to mention Kevin and Amy and the producers and the studios to say, "Hey, let's take a shot at this," - because it's not an easy thing to do.

But if you're gonna keep making these movies you better have something up your sleeve, otherwise it feels repetitive. And I think things have been growing and transforming into new things consistently for over a decade now.

Happy has an impressive condo in *No Way Home*...
It's a nice place, right there on the river in Long Island City looking at Manhattan. Tony Stark probably paid well...

That's the other thing I like: when you see what he's got in storage there, it's all the stuff from all the movies. It kinda mirrors how I feel. I have my memories, and I have my little props from each film. They dug out all these props from all the old films, and what's cool is that Happy is nostalgic about all the events that took place. Even though he's not working for Tony Stark anymore, Tony clearly made a huge impression on him, and here he is surrounded by these memories. People who've seen all the movies or grown up with the films are gonna relate more to Happy. They're gonna think it's cool that he kept all that stuff - you know, the Stark Expo model and posters.

Do you enjoy these films where you can step back from filmmaking and just focus on playing Happy?
As a filmmaker and as a storyteller, you're always learning. I love to watch other filmmakers. You don't get a better seat than acting. So I love to be on other people's sets. Acting takes up a lot of time and the days are long. So if I'm gonna do it, I want to make sure I'm doing it on something that I really believe in and working with people that I really can learn from. Because I think you gotta keep growing, always... Storytelling is one thing, and even though you're wearing different hats, it's all one skill set. Anything you learn in one area applies to others and makes you a better storyteller.

Was there a lot of spontaneity on the set of *No Way Home*?
It's a balance. I think you want to leave room for spontaneity, but you do need to plan. This one was planned very thoroughly. You have to know what can move and what can't because it's so effects driven. All the sets have to be built, the planning has to be done, and all the resources have to be brought to bear. You have to be responsible. You have to take full advantage of the time that you have, the people that are working with you, and not be discovering more than you have to.

However, you do have to find those moments where you can be spontaneous and you can have freedom. One of the reasons I enjoy working with Jon Watts so much is because there's a tremendous amount of freedom within the parameters of what the day's work is. So if we were ever doing something that's technical or if he had a shot that he wanted and he knew exactly what it was, we helped him find it. Even if he was discovering it on his own on the day, we were his paints in his paint box.

When we were doing one scene going through May's apartment, he wanted to do it with a handheld camera with one shot, ripping through three scenes... He was kinda discovering it as we go. That style of filmmaking goes back to my independent film days where you're trying to figure out how to make something exciting and interesting. To see Jon come in with that same degree of freedom and treating this like an independent film for that sequence was really fun.

Then, of course, I love that he has a strong comedy background. He was always letting us improv a few takes on different lines and finding the scene so that we could breathe some humanity and life into those moments. They felt like they flowed better. Again, it's really all in the eye of the filmmaker. It never felt like an overly technical experience. Even when we were doing the action sequences, there was a lot of room for freedom. He managed to find opportunities to stay loose and have discoveries happen even within the more confining aspects of filmmaking.

What was your reaction when you heard that Tobey Maguire and Andrew Garfield were coming back?
I had heard rumors about the casting, and I had also talked to Jon in dribs and drabs. So I was getting only little bits of it. But I had heard what he was gonna do, I was like, "How is he gonna ever do that?"

Next thing I know I'm on the set and he's showing me some early assemblies of all three Spider-Men put together! Now, I met all of them on the sets of their movies because I was sort of floating around the Marvel Studios world throughout all of them. And they're all super nice. And now to see them all in a film together interacting... It just feels really innovative. It feels like a way to explore things in a way that's not repeating itself. It takes a certain amount of courage and playfulness.

The other thing that's really cool was to see and hear how happy and grateful people were to be involved with it. They showed up ready to have a good time and ready to participate in this. It was an exciting notion, and it comes through. I've been involved behind the camera in enough films to recognize how big of an impact it has when everybody's brimming with excitement about making something. In those scenes, you see a lot of that spark come through. It feels like a dream you could've had, where you cross your wires and they're all there together. ☻

J.K. SIMMONS

J. JONAH JAMESON

In Sam Raimi's original *Spider-Man* trilogy, J. Jonah Jameson is the irascible editor of *The Daily Bugle*, while *Far From Home* and *No Way Home* see the character reporting for the sensationalist, Spider-Man-outing website *TheDailyBugle.net*. J.K. Simmons talks about guerilla-style shoots, creative freedom, and finding out he'd been cast as J.J.J.

01

01 Jameson presents his show that revealed the truth about Spider-Man's secret identity.

Did you need to catch up with the events of the Marvel Cinematic Universe?
If my family and I weren't big fans of the movies, then I'd have needed to catch up. But my daughter and my wife and I and – a little less so - my son are big movie fans in general and giant Marvel fans. We've seen every Marvel Studios movie released!

How has the making of a Spider-Man movie changed since the original film?
[This time] my trailer was bigger. That's the main thing that I noticed! It continues to top itself. And, knock on wood, it'll continue to do that.

How would you describe Jon Watts and Sam Raimi's approaches to filmmaking?
What strikes me most about Jon, really, is the ways in which he's similar to Sam. They're both super smart, creative guys, and they're also guys who take such great joy in getting to do this kid stuff for a living and play in this comic book universe.

The thing that struck me about Sam initially, as a less experienced film actor, was he was so prepared on every given day. He knew every second of what he wanted to get. But, as I had learned in my previous two films with him, he was also wide open to having actors improvise and always gave us the opportunity to bring our own sensibility and even our own dialogue to it oftentimes. And it was fun to have that same freedom with Jon [too]. Between the writers and him and me, we just kept throwing stuff at the wall, and then he and the editor decided what stuck… You know, I'm a small cog in this wheel of the Spider-Man universe. But it's nice that everybody was open to listening as to what could be a good idea and going with that old "best idea wins" kind of a vibe.

Why do people connect to J.J.J.?
Well, I'm glad they finally figured out that you can't have Spider-Man without J.J.J.! He is a fun guy for audiences to identify with. Some people say it's the guy you love to hate. I guess you could argue the point that he outed Spider-Man, or more accurately that he outed Peter Parker. The character, to me, will always be a throwback to what Stan Lee and the gang were putting on paper 60 years ago.

Why do you think the MCU is so popular?
I think it's an interesting dichotomy. You think of this as kind of escapist, popcorn movie fun. And it is that, and it checks all those boxes. But almost all these movies now interconnect in such an interesting way, with Spider-Man being sort of a protégé of Iron Man and all the different ways that these Marvel characters interact and show up in each other's stories. And there's a depth to this storytelling. They are entertaining, fun, Super Hero movies, but they have something to say about the human condition and the world as we know it. ☻

Can you remember the moment you found out you'd been cast as J. Jonah Jameson in Sam Raimi's original *Spider-Man*?
It was 1998 or 1999, and I was working on my second movie with Sam Raimi. We had done *For The Love of the Game* together, and the next year we were down in Georgia making *The Gift*. And word got out that Sam was going to be directing the new *Spider-Man* movie. Of course, everybody was excited. My friends started to tell me, "Oh, you should talk to Sam, and you should play the Vulture" - or whatever other bald character exists in the Spider-Man universe. And I never did. Then, a couple of months later, we got the call that Sam wanted me to play J. Jonah Jameson.

Were you surprised to be asked back for *Far From Home* and then *No Way Home*?
It was a complete surprise when I got the call from my agent. And it all came together very quickly. I was just so happy to be back in this world and have fun and get to play in the sandbox.

CHRIS MCKENNA
& ERIK SOMMERS

With *Spider-Man: No Way Home*, writers Chris McKenna and Erik Sommers
have delivered a fresh, funny, and fascinating new twist on
the Super Hero genre. The duo talk about how they went
about combining large-scale action with
small-scale character moments.

Is it difficult to stay true to the spirit of Spider-Man's history while delivering new twists on the formula?

Erik Sommers: It's always a huge challenge to take something from the source material - and there's years and years, decades and decades of it – and bring it to the screen, and try to make it fresh and interesting while also honoring what that source material was. And so with every character, with every storyline, we're all talking about it and really being deliberative about satisfying the fans but also giving them a slightly new twist on the thing that they've seen before or in the comics that are so beloved. It's just a case-by-case basis. How are we going to do it with this character? How would we do it with this story?

Chris McKenna: Jon Watts, the director, always says it's the ground level of the Marvel Cinematic Universe, just be true to that. Peter's always going to have homework. He's always going to have problems with the kids in his class. And he's always going to have relatable teenage problems on top of his Spider-Man problems, but always doing it in a way that feels like he's struggling to just sort of make his way in the Marvel Cinematic Universe. It's a struggle for him because every time he gets a taste of a little bit of victory, he gets knocked back down.

Erik Sommers: The nice thing about working with the folks at Marvel Studios is that they're all fans. They all enjoy the source material. And everyone working on this project from Amy [Pascal] to Jon to us, are fans. We all cherish the source material. And we're all willing to look at those characters in a new light and say, "What are we going to do with this?" And, "Oh, the fans would like that." Why? Because, well, that sounds neat to us. We would love to see that. Hopefully, the fans would like to see that. And so we just take it from there.

In this movie we had an opportunity to have Peter teamed up with Doctor Strange in a way that we'd never done before. And so we got to look at the source material. "Oh, what are some cool stories where they first met? What's the first time they worked together 50 years ago or whatever in that comic? And what would that look like now?" That was really fun.

What impact does Doctor Strange have on Peter's life?

Chris McKenna: I think he's anything but a mentor to Peter in this movie. Peter does go to him for advice and help at a certain point, wondering if there's some way that he can put the genie back in the bottle. And that leads to a series of circumstances, which makes things much, much worse. Doctor Strange is mostly just terribly annoyed with Peter that he's upended his life and that certain things have happened [and] now he's getting dragged into that he wants nothing to do with.

What does Tom Holland bring to the role of Spider-Man?

Erik Sommers: We both come from TV where, if you're lucky, you're writing on a show and you're writing for those characters for seasons. You really get to see the character progress, but you also get to see the actor sort of just imbue that character more and more and really start to take them on. And it becomes so much easier and more enjoyable to write for that character.

The film sees Peter Parker face his biggest challenge yet, doesn't it?

Chris McKenna: He's a hopeful, optimistic character. That's what's great about Peter. No matter how badly things go, he really hopes that he can pull it off... But, really, that optimism is sort of shining through. He does think that he can somehow get through this and weather this storm. And, well, he might be wrong!

Erik Sommers: One of the big challenges always for Spider-Man has been juggling his duties as Spider-Man and his life as Peter Parker, which is a secret life. The people don't know he's Spider-Man. Trying to keep that separate and secret, trying to keep those people safe - that's something that's been dealt with in the universe of Spider-Man since the beginning. But with this movie we get to start in a place where that has all been completely upended. Now everybody knows. Half the world thinks he's guilty of some crime, and he has to deal with the same problems he's always had but in this much more heightened and chaotic environment.

Chris McKenna: When we ended the last movie we were like, "Wow, we really blew things up. How are the next writers gonna get out of that jam?" And now here we are.

Erik Sommers: Yeah, we did this to ourselves.

01 Spider-Man and MJ on the run.

▶ That's absolutely the opportunity we've had working on these *Spider-Man* films to see Tom Holland, who is such a good actor, just jump into the skin of Peter Parker and make that character his own. It's a joy to have an actor who's that good and to sort of have a feel for where he's been and how the character is progressing.

Chris McKenna: I think there's such an earnestness and sweetness and good-heartedness that he just projects. Also, I think he's an amazing comedic actor. I know he's been compared to a young Michael J. Fox before. He's able to exude that kind of intelligence, yet earnestness, but can just land comic reactions. He's so fun to write for because in my mind it's so hard for me to even separate him at this point from Peter Parker. He just fully embodies Peter Parker to me.

Erik Sommers: He's so youthful, yet he has this physicality. So you really buy him as someone who is essentially a nerd, but when he's also doing his own stunts and everything there on-screen, you realize, "Oh, that's a nerd who is also a Super Hero." And then, of course, Spider-Man is an underdog. Tom has such an earnest energy about him, and he's just a perfect person to play everyone's favorite underdog.

The supporting characters are an important part of these films, aren't they?

Chris McKenna: Absolutely, because obviously from the beginning he's a teenager in high school and he has teenage problems and he has teenage friends. He's just learning how to deal with life while also as this alter ego wrestling literally with villains. So from the beginning in *Homecoming*, they put together these great characters surrounding Peter.

It's so relatable because we all went to high school, and we all had friends and crushes. And [we] get to work with those great characters like MJ and Ned and Betty and Flash, [and] keep on making a richer, intimate world for Peter, and also give him personal stakes.

Erik Sommers: I think one of the things that has always drawn people to Spider-Man is that he's this high school kid just trying to figure it out… Whenever people tell me they liked [*Far From Home*], the first thing they talk about is all the fun of Peter and his friends on that school trip. Then all of a sudden Spider-Man stuff happens. And so we were excited to take that into this new dynamic where his identity is out in the open and everyone knows, and how that affected them as well. It gave us such an opportunity to explore those characters in a new light.

Chris McKenna: Now that everything is out in the open, they get a real insight and a direct effect of what it's like to be Peter Parker because now they are being recognized… There is a lot of the elements of, "What if you became best friends with a world-renowned celebrity, who in some people's eyes is a bad guy?" So they have to deal with that too.

We had a lot of fun with just organically playing off of the events from the last movie, and how these characters would react to all of this. Can they have a normal teenage life? Can they all go off to college together? Is there any world where that can happen? Or is that a pipe dream?

02 Spider-Man defies Doctor Strange as he steals the spell that sends the villains back to their universes.

03 Peter shows his ingenuity as he turns his suit inside out before his battle with Electro.

04 Norman Osborn battles Peter Parker.

You always balance big stakes with small character moments, don't you?

Chris McKenna: Peter's emotional state is always what's really driving his stories, and that's what's so great and human about him.

Erik Sommers: Whenever I talk to people about the movies, they might mention some element of plot or something cool the villain did or some of the action or something. But the thing that always really sticks with them is whatever emotional story happened for Peter during the movie, whatever change he underwent, him getting together with MJ or something exciting.

That's what people remember really, what sticks with them. And so we're always thinking about that.

How did you manage to make the characters so down-to-earth and relatable?

Chris McKenna: We were writers on *Marvel Studios' Ant-Man and The Wasp*, which came right after *Marvel Studios' Avengers: Infinity War*. And one of the mantras for us was: it can be small. It can be small and fun and funny, because we were coming off this giant thing. Then we were writing *Far From Home* [and] we were given basically the same mantra.

You can have fun with it. It doesn't have to be huge… It's funny. I mean, yes, they're big in their own ways. And, obviously, *Far From Home* has huge things in it, but to us that just means in a way, "Oh, we can just really try to drill down as much on character."

Erik Sommers: Character moments… just that ground-level stuff that people really enjoy in these movies.

Chris McKenna: It's trying to write honestly about, "OK, how would this character that we've all grown to love, what would happen if…?" How does Peter respond to this, realistically, honestly? There is big fallout from what he's done, but it all comes to a place [where] he just wishes that certain things could go back to the way they were. And he's also haunted by the death of Mysterio, because not only does he resent everything that's happened but he also feels really guilty. Spider-Man doesn't kill people. At the end of *Homecoming*, he goes into flames to save the bad guy. He doesn't want Vulture to die. He wants to save him. And that's the goodhearted person that he is. He's the kind of hero who doesn't like villains to die on his watch. Mysterio died. And he's haunted by that idea…

Erik Sommers: With the first two movies we knew we wanted to really lean into that ground-level MCU kind of stuff - that very relatable, street-level Spider-Man viewpoint of the MCU and dig into the characters. We didn't necessarily feel pressured to make it gigantic in scope and scale because the *Marvel Studios' Avengers* movies were happening and everything. This time around we wanted to dig into that same stuff and really enjoy Peter and his friends and all those characters, and follow through on everything we'd set up in the other two, but go much bigger in the scope of what happens. ☻

> ## "Peter's emotional state is always what's really driving his stories…"
> ## — Chris McKenna

How did you approach developing MJ and Ned in this film?

Chris McKenna: MJ is a pretty tough and a pretty loyal character. And she's a really great ally for Peter to help him try to get through this especially rough period of his life. Then things take a turn that make it even tougher, but Peter's friends are always there for him. They help him on this journey throughout the movie and put their own lives at risk, knowingly and willingly to try to help him deal with this insane situation that he's gotten himself into.

Erik Sommers: I mean, what's it like for MJ to go from being Peter Parker's girlfriend to suddenly being the girlfriend of the guy who is the most famous person on Earth and who some people think is a criminal? What is it like for Ned to go from being proud "guy in the chair" to his friend Peter to "guy in the chair" to someone who has been accused of these horrible crimes. And [he's] now an accomplice, you know? What is it like for Flash, who doesn't particularly like Peter Parker, but is a huge fan of Spider-Man, to suddenly discover that they're the same person? How is he going to handle that news?

SET DESIGN, DECORATION & PROPS

No Way Home's art department was responsible for everything from recreating New York City in Atlanta to filling Doctor Strange's basement with arcane artifacts and constructing the villains' weapons. We talk to production designer Darren Gilford, set decorator Rosemary Brandenburg, and property master Russell Bobbitt.

PRODUCTION DESIGN
DARREN GILFORD

How close to reality did you want the production design on *No Way Home* to be?
Jon Watts wanted it to feel very real and based in reality. Even with these wild fantasy elements, he loved to ground them and bring them back so they didn't go too far off the rails. That's always great because it helps me kind of stay in my lane!

How important was it to incorporate practical elements into the design?
We always fight to have as much represented in front of the camera as we can. Every filmmaker, every director of photography I've ever worked with needs that. The visual effects supervisors as well; they want as much information as they can get. Even if it's a small amount of a surface, at least they understand how light's hitting it, how it's interacting, how the bounce is happening, how the colors are… That translates not only for visual effects but for the performances. As soon as an actor has something they can interact with, it grounds them.

How do you plan visual effects into your designs?
I started as a digital effects art director. I was attracted to this business because I wanted to design environments that couldn't be built originally. I was fascinated at this void that I saw between traditional production and visual effects, and I wanted to be a designer that could bridge the gap between those two things. For example, the Statue of Liberty – it was an erector set of scaffolding. But we only built small pieces of the actual Statue of Liberty. Understanding how big the statue is to the scaffolding and figuring out where all these actors have to swing through or fly around is the fun.

Can you talk about designing Happy's condo?
Happy was such a fun character to dive into and figure out what his world would be like post-Tony Stark. There's a little bit of melancholy there. We didn't want it to be too sad, but we didn't want it to be too extravagant or over the top. Thinking about Happy, [we were] trying to figure out his social class within the city. We didn't want him to feel like he inherited tremendous wealth from Tony. We wanted to make it feel like he's a working- class guy…We put Happy's apartment in

Long Island City. We didn't want him in the center of Manhattan in this crazy, spacious high-rise. We wanted him a little out of the city... Finding that right kind of balance is everything, from materials and the appliances to the colors and the fabrics. One of the requirements was, "What if everything was bought out of an airplane magazine?" The couch, the coffee maker, everything in the place. We thought that was a good sensibility.

Happy's relationship with May was so much fun to play off of. I wanted to have absolutely no feminine influences in the beginning when we first saw it. So when [May and Peter] do move in and Marisa comes in with all of her stuff, it's a great contrast between this very masculine sensibility and this sudden influx of May's flair!

Did you want to include many nods to his time with Tony Stark?
There's a huge mural of Tony's hot-rod, a '34 Ford Coupe. We hired a well-known automotive artist to do a classic Bonneville Salt Flat painting of Tony's original car... Maybe this is one of the things that Happy took with him as a memory of Tony. Subtle things like that. We

didn't want to make it this crazy tribute to Tony, but we wanted to have a few things in there that touched on his past.

Did you conduct research for iconic sets like the Statue of Liberty?
I looked at all the Statue of Liberty reference movies. Also, we went through the whole Library of Congress restoration project on the Statue of Liberty to understand the special equipment and rigging and scaffolding. That was great reference because we could actually get really close to surfaces of the statue that you could never get to unless you were on those types of structures.

I did look at all those old movies [that feature the statute]. *Remo Williams* is a great example. They had to build everything back then. That was long before modern-day visual effects. We do things a bit differently now just for an efficiency level for how much stuff we have to do and how fast we've got to move, but I definitely researched all that stuff. We got to actually build the head of the Statue of Liberty, which was really fun. We had an incredible sculpting team that sculpted it by hand and did an amazing job with the crown.

01 Tom Holland on the basement set of Doctor Strange's home on Bleeker Street.

02 Peter and MJ explore the cellar.

03 Peter confronts Norman Osborn on the Statue of Liberty.

▶ How did the idea of Lady Liberty holding Cap's shield arise?

We explored a lot of different options. We thought maybe the shield was on her back. Then we put her holding the shield on her wrist, and maybe she was still holding the torch... We knew we wanted to restore the copper. That was really important. We wanted to make her shiny again. We thought that would be a big graphic change visually. The golden, beautiful tones could bounce off of that in the night sky and the scaffolding.

The big event of the shield tearing through the scaffolding and landing in the water was a huge part of our design consideration as well. One of the biggest production issues was on the shield because it was going to be in water and we built it out of real metal... We built it complete and undestroyed. Then, obviously, it was going to be damaged when it comes down. So I had giant backhoe machines on stage crushing and messing the shield up in a certain way, then we welded it back together to make it safe.

We had it in the water for about a week. Because of the chemicals in the water, we had to make it safe for our actors. About two days before we were about to shoot, all the paint just started to peel off of it and rise to the surface of the water. There was some sort of chemical reaction between the heat of the water, the chlorine, and the fact we had crushed the metal... We had to go back, drain it really quick, sand it all down, seal it again, figure out a better way to seal it and put it back down. At the time those are major catastrophes you're scrambling to figure it out. But in the scope of things, that was a small price to pay for a pretty smoothly run production!

Can you talk about the design of the Sanctum?

We had to recreate the big, round circular rotunda foyer, which has been built multiple times on multiple continents at this point. We were lucky because we had tons of drawings, and we had to break it all down. We got to cover it in snow; conceptualizing that was really fun as well. Early on, it was potentially a torrential downpour. One of my ideas was I wanted to have swallows or starlings that whip around in shapes within the room. Then we locked into the snow and a giant portal being opened up and blowing in. The most fun for me was the workshop and the ancient chamber below, which we'd never seen before... The idea was that the ancient chamber is a ruin that was here before New York was even built. If you look closely, we have a beautiful hieroglyphic threshold that opens up into the ancient chamber. It was really important for us to have depth and height.

You used virtual reality in your designs, didn't you?

This was the first movie I've done where I designed a lot of these big sets in virtual reality, which was amazingly fun. I was able to build those sets, put on the headset and show Jon, and walk around and really find our angles... I also did that with the Statue of Liberty, which was amazing. We built the full Statue of

04

05

> "It's important for the actors to have the opportunity to grow into it as they walk around the set."
> — Rosemary brandenburg

04 Sandman enjoys the hospitality at the Parker's apartment.

05 Doctor Strange's domain: the Sanctum Sanctorum set.

Liberty model in the computer, ported it to the Unreal Engine [immersive game engine]. Then it's like a video game. Put the headset on, and we could fly completely around the Statue of Liberty and find our angles! It was a game changer.

How did you go about recreating New York in Atlanta?
We were expecting to go to New York for a big part of our shoot. But as the pandemic developed, we had to shift focus and figure out a new way to do a lot of that work. We had to really recreate a lot of things [in Atlanta].

There were elements like the outside of the high school, which is a pretty simple thing to get in New York. But because we couldn't go there, we had to literally recreate the front of a school in an alley between two soundstages... And we found a gutted store and built the donut shop, which was fantastic. It worked out really well. May's charity was another location that we found locally, and that worked out really well. Most of the other stuff - the city street stuff and the exterior streets of the Sanctum - they shot traditionally in [Greenwich] Village [in New York City].

Can you talk about the design of the fabricator?
It suddenly became a real focal point in our story that would help drive our cures forward. So we had to design it and get it manufactured fairly quickly when we realized our schedule. It was one of the things I dived into personally... I started designing it with some new software, which is in VR in 3D. I had a headset on, I had my hand controls, and I was actually designing this fabricator in the computer... I was like Tony Stark in the *Iron Man* films, interacting with some of the holograms!

SET DECORATION
ROSEMARY BRANDENBURG

How did you update the decor of the Sanctum?
We had the opportunity to do the basement, which had never been done before. That was really fun because we were playing with magic around the edges and an average basement in the middle. It's a surprise to the audience as they first go down and see a very ordinary, junk-filled basement with a Ping-Pong table and an old train set and Christmas decorations from Christmases gone by. Then when you look into the edges you realize there's alchemy going on, and there's a forge for making crazy potions and fixing crazy relics.

▶

▶ We riffed on some of that stuff to find artifacts from Africa and South America and from the Pacific Islands, all kinds of interesting things. And then looking into old magic research: what is alchemy? What did they use? What are the tools? How is it done? How does a concoction get made in a lab setup? It was heavily detailed. Every one of our cast members who came down there had fun poking around the edges!

What does a tangible environment do for a film?
It's really important for [actors] to have an opportunity to really grow into it as they walk into a set and feel the backstory of their character that we've thought up for them. Many of them ad-lib with some of the items that we provide between us and props. I've done a lot of films with huge amounts of blue screen and volume stages, and they all want set dressing. They want that foreground element to play off of. Our job has not diminished. It remains just as serious and just as complete as it was before they even thought of blue screen…

I like to be complete with the backstory that I'm creating and have a tale told through the objects that I provide and how they're arranged. There's a story behind everything that somebody put on that shelf or [why] somebody decided to have that train set or Ping-Pong table down there.

How difficult was it to recreate New York City?
New York is a character in the film. We're in Manhattan. We're in SoHo. We're in Queens. We're in Long Island City. There are very specific things about all of those places that we tried to pay attention to, whether it was the style of a street lamp or the kind of fire hydrant or newspaper boxes or stickers or graffiti. Whether it was an upscale neighborhood or a middle-class neighborhood.

We did a downtown street in Atlanta pretending to be New York. You'd be surprised how much work goes into creating those storefronts and making sure that there's the proper kind of feeling about an ethnic fruit store or a beauty shop or a laundromat, all those things that we did down there. We spent a lot of time doing research and figuring out how to recreate it. Everything from graphics to benches and bus stops and the kind of trash cans and the kind of trash.

How do you go about matching decor to a character?
The character is super important. Like, who is Happy? Who is May? Who is J. Jonah Jameson? Who are these people that have these environments? You think about it a lot. In this case, we had seen their characters, so we kind of had an idea who they were. The Marvel Studios team gave us a lot to go on for Happy, for example, but they wanted him very stark, not a whole lot of stuff… What was in it had to be very specific. We riffed off of a little line [in *Marvel Studios' Iron Man 3*] when he was in the hospital and was watching *Downton Abbey*. So we had *Downton Abbey* DVDs. And he said he had been a boxer in his younger days. We had some boxing gloves and boxing trophies, but they were very tucked away… It was trying to figure out what a bachelor guy like that would [have].

06 Peter, Ned, and MJ survey the captured villains.

"We could dig deep into the archives of the big warehouses where all the props go..."

PROPS
RUSSELL BOBBITT

Why are practical props important?
What's really awesome is that our industry has held onto the creative process. We're still able to design a prop, even though we know it might end up in a CG world or on a CG character. They still rely on us to design it both on paper and deliver it physically. It might need a little help in post-production with the color or the size, perhaps, because it's an ongoing process in developing [prop designs] that might be in a CG shot.

Did you rewatch the old *Spider-Man* movies?
I certainly watched all the films, and we communicated with the other art teams [on other Marvel Studios films]... It's a constant collaboration between prop masters, art departments, as well as us doing our own research as to what has been seen on camera before. We could dig deep into the archives of the big warehouses where all the props go... Most of all, we spoke to the actors and the director about how can it be better? How can it change?

Can you talk about the web shooters?
You always want to riff off of the one that you saw in the last film or the film before that. In this iteration, we learned what was quirky about the first two. If it was a little bit uncomfortable for the actor or if it wasn't shiny enough or we wanted to dull it down, we played with all those aspects. On this film, we introduced a new web shooter that comes out of Doctor Strange's world. For that reason, we had the pleasure of [both] redesigning web shooters and designing new ones.

How did you go about updating props from the earlier films?
The audience expects to see new technology. The trick is to show that new technology in a recognizable fashion - like, "Wow, that's a web shooter. But it's really cool!" We used 3D printing instead of the technology that we had 20 years ago. And paint finishes and the materials that we use are different now. It's an ever-changing evolution of marrying old school with new-school technology.

07 A crate from Stark Industries.

08 Ned enjoys exploring Doctor Strange's collection of artifacts.

Can you talk about Doctor Strange's spell?
It was an ever-changing, evolving prop. We were in constant design. Our prop on the set was green. Because it was ever-changing, it became a computer generated prop. It's a great example of how can we physically help the actors with their spatial relationships in a prop, passing it back and forth, throwing it. We got to a place of where, "This is what it should be in our physical world and we're going to constantly develop it in our computer generated world."

Then there were the cures...
Those were exciting to develop with Jon. Those really key, important props go through many iterations. We drew them eight, ten, twelve times - completely different concepts - until we came down to what we ended up building.

How did you go about updating the villains' iconic props?
We wanted to reintroduce the villains in a very recognizable state. So they all came back with what we know of them - Doc Ock with his mechanical arms, Green Goblin's glider and pumpkin bombs, and so on. We wanted it to be as if time stood still... You might see

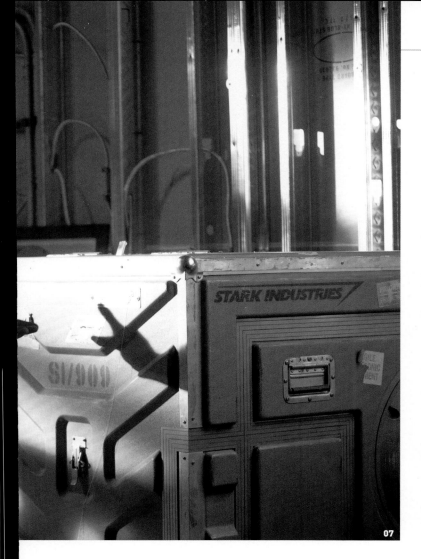

a weapon come off of Goblin's arm that he uses now in this film that he never had before, but it was part of his old technology. We enhanced it a little, but basically riffed off where we last saw them.

What about Electro's arc reactor?
It was tricky because the original design had the arc reactor in the chest [of Tony Stark], and we wanted to make sure it wasn't too close to that... So we immediately took the arc reactor out from the center of the chest and put it up [higher on the chest] so it didn't look like a new Iron Man suit. The creative, fun elements of that suit were insanely challenging to come up with. It's a whole bunch of equipment to put on the actor, but Jamie Foxx was just a dream come true for a costume like that. So patient, loving, and fun. The costume was hard to get on him because he was constantly dancing and listening to music!

Tell us about collaborating with Jon Watts.
Jon Watts is an incredible collaborator. It's rare for a project to be completely 100% organized and ready to go, but Jon adds that. He really has in his mind what it should be. For us, picking his brain and bringing out what's in his mind in conversation is a truly incredible aspect. It adds to the project tremendously because there is no guesswork. He knows if the takeout food should be Thai or Chinese or a hamburger. It's an easy question for him to answer. ●

08

GEORGE COTTLE
STUNTS

George Cottle has been the stunt coordinator on Jon Watts's three Spidey movies, as well as over a hundred other movies and TV shows. He explains how he worked with the cast and crew to ensure that *No Way Home*'s wirework, fights and acrobatics were both awe-inspiring and believable.

How do the stunts and action sequences in *No Way Home* differ than the previous films?

The fights are a lot more aggressive than in the previous movies. There's a lot more to lose in this movie from Peter's point of view, and I think that really shows in the action and the fights we put together.

When we first got on board with this show, we realized all of the villains that were gonna be in it, [and knew that] we had to bring something new and something fresh to the table with those guys. We didn't just have to bring good action and work out what direction we wanted to take Peter Parker and Spider-Man, but we also had to break down the action and the look of the bad guys.

What did you do physically differentiate the different Spider-Men?

I lucked out. I've had the same team with me for the last four or five shows. And one of my guys on this team, Chris Daniels, who's my head rigger, was the Tobey double for the first three Spideys... It was a huge insight for us to have his knowledge and ability of what actually went down on those movies.

Then the two other members of my team were the doubles for Andrew on the other two Spideys! And, obviously, we had the guys who were the doubles for Tom on the two new Spideys [films], Greg and Luke. We then parlayed that into my fight coordinator, Jackson Spidell, who's a huge Marvel comic book fan. We put it all in the pot, tried to keep the tradition of what the fights and the bad guys would normally focus on alive but also put our spin on it.

I think when you're playing in the world of three Spideys, you have to be very respectful of each individual Spidey. We had to really study the unique looks of every Spidey and make sure that we never crossed over. So whenever we were bringing a Spidey into a scene or having them up on wires and landing them in a scene, they all had their very unique looks and unique form. We had to make sure we stayed true to that.

Did you work closely with Tobey and Andrew on their action scenes?

Oh, absolutely. I mean, we got Tom for a nice amount of rehearsal time and we'd done the last two movies with Tom. So we had a really good base understanding of what Tom wanted... But with Tobey and Andrew, we only had them for a short window. So a lot of the stuff we were doing, and a lot of the communications about what they wanted to achieve and what action ▶

STUNS

they were specifically looking for, was pretty much based around their conversation with Jon Watts. Then Jon would come to me and he'd be like, "Look, I think this, this, this." So we would put the rehearsal videos [of] the fight stuff together prior to them getting here. Jon would then present it to them, and they would be like, "I like this, I don't like this." We would break that down specifically for whether it'd be Tobey, Andrew, or Tom.

That even played out on the day when we were doing some of the end battle sequence and when they first arrived in the movie. In the scene where they have a standoff and do unique Spidey tricks, we had to make sure that whatever the move was, however small, that it really played well to their character and was something their Spidey would actually do and not something that, say, Tom would've done in *Homecoming*.

Were the other actors excited about the stunts?
One hundred percent. I mean, Willem is just a gent. He worked so hard. He would turn up to rehearsals [and] we would put him in a harness. He is still in incredible shape. He phoned me up prior to this movie and was like, "I just want to let you know I want to do as much as possible. Please don't count me out." He was a trooper…

Alfred Molina, because he moves around on the legs so much, we had him in a harness for 90% of the time that he was working with us. He was a rock star! He did absolutely phenomenal stuff, up and around on blue screen [with] the guys puppeteering him. Those harnesses aren't the most comfortable things in the world. Obviously, we try to do everything we can to make them as comfortable as possible. But, you know, I wouldn't want to be spending the hours that they're spending in those things, and I'm in that department!

How difficult was the wirework?
The hard thing was at some point we had to put six, seven, even eight characters on wires at the same time. But we also had to make sure they had their own individual feeling, their own individual movement, and they had to be very unique to their own character. That was one of the biggest challenges. We couldn't just hang Doc Ock there and hang the Green Goblin there because they move very differently. And Goblin moves around on his flyer. So we had to make sure that when we were doing wires with him, that it played uniquely to his movements and his character.

Can you talk about the fight in Happy's condo?
That is probably one of my favorite sequences in the whole movie… The difference with the Green Goblin [compared to other villains] is that he is super strong. He can take the violence from Spidey. That was a really interesting and exciting avenue for us to explore. So from very early on when we started putting the fights together, we didn't have to worry [in terms of realism] about Spidey just punching him straight in the jaw. Or Spidey punching him in the stomach and worrying about breaking every rib in his body. This was something the Goblin could take. Not only could he take it, he could give it back as good as he was getting. That was really fun for us to explore.

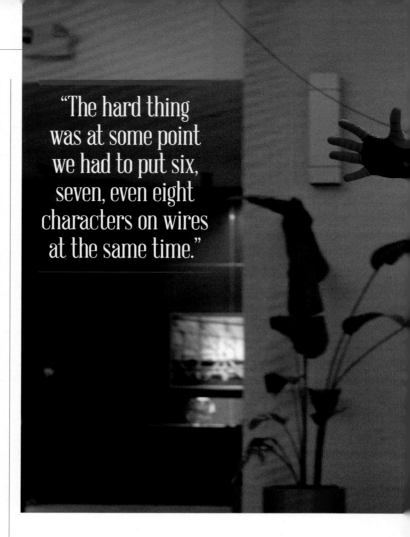

> "The hard thing was at some point we had to put six, seven, even eight characters on wires at the same time."

I remember one of the sequences in the corridor where Spidey isn't doing so good in the fight. It's kinda his last-ditch effort. He's got Goblin pinned against the wall, and he's giving it all he can. Willem is just doing these incredible reactions with his face and then stops and gives the Goblin cackle. Everybody on set just stopped. It kinda made your hair stand on end. It was just so iconic and amazing and perfectly timed.

Can you talk about the climactic shield fight?
Spidey got a little bit of a beating in Happy's condo. So it sets us up really well for another match. It's kind of the Apollo Creed/Rocky rematch in *Rocky II*, where you hope things are gonna go better… Tom [Holland's Spider-Man] has got so much hatred, he is just ready to tear his arms and legs off at this point. So much of that fight had to be raw aggression and pure anger. But we also know he has to hold his temper or else that's gonna be the one thing that lets him down… Everybody really worked hard to make the fight as brutal and as heartfelt as you hoped it would be.

One of the finishing moves in the fight, which Jackson came up with and I really loved, was Tom doing a front handspring over the back of Goblin, using his hands – because they're sticky - to flick him over his head and smash him into the floor… When we did it on the day, there was one moment where [stunt double] Greg is swinging him

01 Spider-Man takes MJ on a hair-raising ride through the city.

02 Tom Holland brings 110% to his athletic performance as Spider-Man.

round and slams him on the floor so hard that Greg's feet lifted off the floor. It just plays so well to that last ditch effort of [Spider-Man giving] everything he's got into trying to take him out. That was one of my favorite shots.

Why is Jon a great director for Spider-Man?
Jon was kind enough to let me direct second unit. One of the key things about the working relationship I have with Jon is that I like to think that I bring the high energy cool action, but he's so fantastic at bringing the acting and the emotional side of where he wants his movie to go into my world… It was crucial for us to have that friendship and that ability to go back and forward over everything that we shot together.

How did Zendaya approach her stunts?
The first day we had Zendaya with us, it was supposed to be her jumping off a bridge in New York for the opening sequence. Day one, we had her in, we had a scissor lift 55 feet in the air. We had two hundred-foot cranes above her, and Spidey grabs her, and off she goes. I said to Z, "Do you want to rehearse?" She was like, "No, I'm good. I trust you. Just tell me where to be and I'll be there…" And take one she nailed it. It was just incredible. We had the camera right next to her on a high-speed winch. She did nearly 50 feet of freefall and nine feet of deceleration to her mark. And absolutely perfect!

She is just incredibly talented, and she has really fantastic spatial awareness and body awareness, which is crucial because when she's falling it's not like she's falling on her own. She's falling with Spidey right next to her, so she has to remember to keep her arm in the right place and hold this arm in the right place. And we have to get that moment. Not only are they bringing the stunt side of this into the equation, they have to act on top!

Can you explain how you work with Tom Holland on the stunts?
We know each other very well, and in a way I consider him to be like my little brother. For someone at 26 years of age to have such a commanding presence on a set is truly incredible. He really set the tone for the movie. He was always in great spirits. He would always say hi and good morning to everybody. And he led the charge.

Between him and Jon Watts, they brought 110% every single day. As tired as you felt on some of the days, when you saw that energy and that passion, it just made you want to do better. It made you work harder… He would literally go until there was nothing left in his body. When we did the last couple of takes when he was fighting Willem, he would just drop to the floor when they called "cut". He was spent. There was nothing left. And the next day he would come to work, and he would be ready to go. ☻

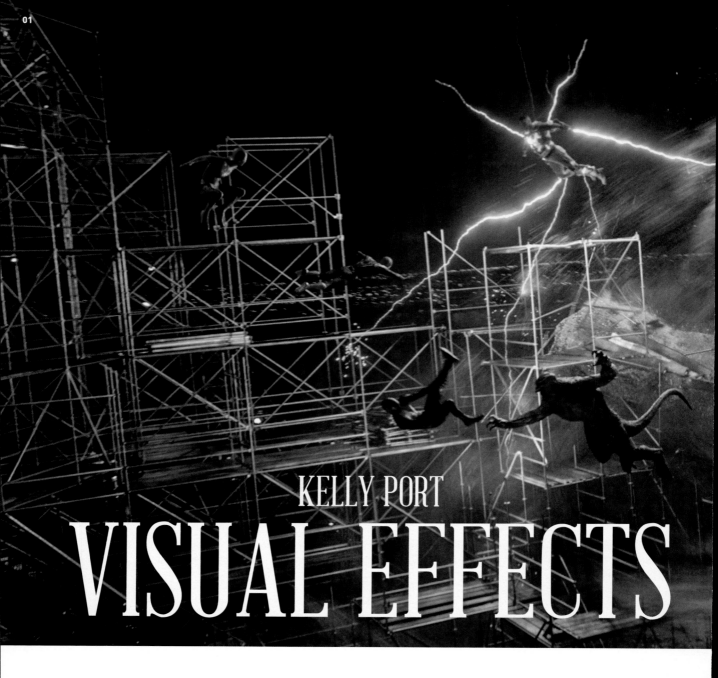

KELLY PORT
VISUAL EFFECTS

Visual effects supervisor Kelly Port was charged with overseeing *Spider-Man: No Way Home*'s staggeringly ambitious VFX shots, from Doctor Strange's spells to the Sandman forming himself from the ground. He explains how he made the impossible possible.

Did you use any visual effects materials from the Tobey Maguire and Andrew Garfield movies?

Certain aspects. Interestingly, for a lot of the digital characters from the Raimi and Webb films, we weren't able to get those assets. So for those we had to get going from scratch. However, there were some practical things that we had access to. For example, Doc Ock's arms, which we rescanned and took lots of additional reference photography. We noticed in analyzing the previous films that there were different looks of those arms from shot to shot. It was like, "Oh, this is interesting. This is different. This wasn't in this shot, which one do we use?" So we kind of had to settle on something and

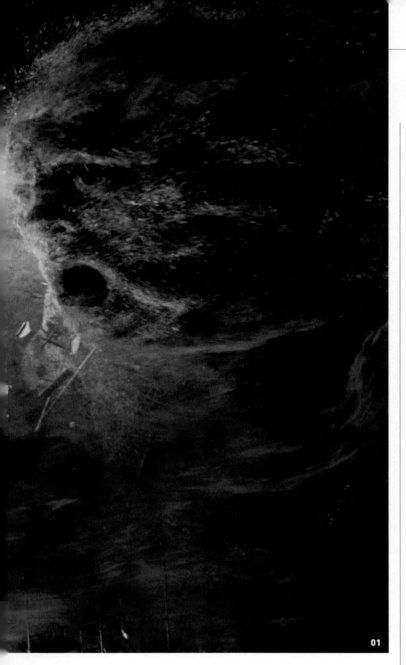

How true did you stay to the web-shooters from the earlier films?

We wanted to try to up it in terms of quality. But those webs in the previous films look pretty good. Often times, [we were like] "Okay, let's just start with that." Then if we needed a hero shot of it, we made some technical adjustments. A lot of times in the end battle, it was all pretty quick and wide.

A couple of the villains are entirely digital, aren't they?

For Sandman, this is true. He was gonna always be 100% digital. I had a lot of really interesting discussions about how he moved. For example, how does Sandman go from A to B? If you're made out of sand, is the most practical, efficient way to get across the living room floor to make yourself into a human shape and walk? Or would you just sort of blow over there? And then if you need to talk, how does that work? Does he create vocal cords made out of sand? There were all sorts of interesting things... I liked this idea that he's always sort of shape-shifting, that he's always this sort of flowing sand.

A similar thing with Electro. At the beginning, when we first see him, we were playing with him as pure energy, largely. He can be quite large. He can be small. He can be anything he wants. There are small electrical feelers that go out. He can jump. What's really interesting is that he can get into action poses and fights and power moves, but he doesn't have to obey his own physical space. He can throw a punch, but that punch can go through his own body... I loved this idea of playing with how electricity behaves in this staccato kind of animation. That he could be right in front of you and then he could be there or there or there. It throws his adversaries off guard. But we also wanted to see Jamie Foxx. So I liked this idea that he can decide when he wants to visualize himself in a more human way, but also part of his physicality can be pure energy at times as well.

Is it difficult to create the texture of a character like Sandman?

When we first encounter him, he's in the forest in dirt. I loved this idea that, yes, he's made out of sand, but he can kinda control or pick up parts of the earth too, so he's not just this fine-grained, perfect beach sand guy. He actually picks up some texture in the dirt - some twigs and rocks and dirt clods and things like that gave some more interesting visual texture to it.

How did you create the Lizard?

This is one of those areas where visual effects has made tremendous progress year after year in making those kinds of surfaces look more and more real... [Head of visual development] Ryan Meinerding and his team always do such a great job with conceptualizing these characters. I think it looks pretty damn cool!

make it ours. That worked fine, because we were doing a new thing with the nanotechnology seeping in. That was something new that we were playing with.

But ours [Doc Ock's tentacles] was based primarily on the physical prop that [Sony] had in their archive, so we started with that. [Special effects supervisor] Dan Sudick and his team milled it and created amazing lighting reference that we could use on any shot, both with the nano and without. We had two different lighting references that would come out at the end of a particular setup and we could rotate it around to see how it looked in a particular lighting environment.

So essentially, we based it on that. It was a bunch of repeating joints. Then digitally we created additional substructure and mechanisms for how it worked to make it cooler and more complicated but still living and true to the original as much as possible.

01 Battle at the Statue of Liberty as the villains duel three Spider-Men!

Is it exciting to see character designs from Ryan and his ream?
It's so fun to be a part of that, to see those kinds of things, because he and his team are just so talented. To see these iconic images... he always puts them in these fantastic poses and in an environment that looks so epic. It's really fun just to be a part of that initial presentation.

Can you talk about the Green Goblin glider?
A large part of it was CG. But for the photography him flying on it, there was a gimbal created by Dan Sudick and his team, which he could ride and the stunt guys could fight on... What we did was just offset it a little, so rather than it being static the way they filmed it - not necessarily moving in time with how he would have been manipulating the [glider] and the wings – we would slide him a little bit over or forward and make those connections work.

How did you go about creating *No Way Home*'s version of the Statue of Liberty?
It was a little bit of a mix. The island itself was fully digital, aside from the set pieces that we built, which were extended digitally. The water [around] the island was digital as well. But [for] the deep background, like the cityscape, we had a location team led by Chris Buongiorno that did

helicopter plates at night and day... They shot plates so you got a full 360 view.

Did you go back and look at the classic comics?
We did. Sometimes for easter eggs and nods to the comics... For example, [the moment] with Electro having that iconic star around his head. [We asked] "How do you realize that in a photographic realistic way?" It was something we wanted to do, but it had to be tasteful and look photorealistic too.

How did you go about creating the visual effects for Doctor Strange's spells?
I think that was probably one of the bigger challenges because it's so important to find that language of the magic... It needs to tell you something is happening. We had a vision for what it was, and when we had Doctor Strange in the Sanctum chamber, we had some interactive light [on set] because we know that these little pieces of magic, whatever that they are, are luminous. They light up the world [while] he and Peter Parker and are rotating. And he's doing his hand gestures, and is channeling his energy and basically writing a spell of magic around the room. Then this gets increasingly

"You plan, but you also plan to have everything change from under you..."

02 Spider-Man's Stark-enhanced armor features CGI arms.

03 Sorcerer Vs web-slinger!

chaotic, and so the interactive lights we had on set had to get increasingly chaotic.

Then we did some concept images of, "OK, what could that be?" I would show that to Jon, and he'd give me a few different variations of it and say [things] like, "That's the right idea, but I want it more cursive. I want it connected, more like a line or multiplied." Or "Let's lose some of it on top." We also had a background color that was almost like neurons, but was soft and faded. It was cyan kind of deep, and showed off the deep caverns of the ancient chamber. It gave some color contrast to the more orangey-red magic. It was sort of this step-by-step process. Then we started seeing it animated and seeing it within the shots, cut together and roughed in.

Were there physical props that stood in for artefacts that were created in CGI, like the box containing Doctor Strange's spells?
Yeah, everyone carried around this wooden painted green box with orange tracking dots on it!

You used multiple VFX companies on the film, didn't you?
We hire visual effects studios, give them the right amount of work and hopefully if it grows or changes they can accommodate that. We want to be able to continue to develop the images creatively and be able to change it all the way up until the end…

We had multiple vendors for different characters [and they] could bounce stuff off each other. It's actually nice to have a couple different groups going at it from different creative angles. Then you can share, "Oh look, these guys did this. This is a really cool idea." We developed a language in order to communicate creatively. For example, with Electro there were "reachers," "outlines," "surface fade." They were all things that equated to a visual representation of electricity. [As opposed to] saying, "Well, can you make him look a little bit more *bzzzt?*"

How much of your work changes at the last minute?
You plan, but you also plan to have everything change from under you… You want to have an idea how you're gonna shoot something or how you approach something and you try to feed images to the powers that be - Jon, Kevin, everybody who made those final decisions. But at the end of the day - and this is what Kevin has always said - it's about making it the best story as possibly it can be. If that required completely changing out an environment or a costume at the last minute, we had to be prepared to do that. ☻

HAIR, MAKEUP & COSTUMES

No Way Home's hair, costume and makeup departments worked closely together to subtly update the look of the much-loved characters. Hair department head Linda Flowers, costume designer Sanja Hays, and makeup department head Vasilios Tanis reveal some of the secrets of their craft.

HAIR

How important is the characters' hair to the story?
Linda Flowers: It's very important. It can tell a story. It can tell us about a period, a time, what somebody's going through emotionally. And this is [set] in New York, where the people have a very definite style. They're casual yet always done [up]. I think hair can take you someplace.

I always keep that in mind when I read the script. Like, how do I want to be a part of this narrative? What can I do with the hair to take people where they need to go, location-wise or time period-wise?

How do you approach a sequel?
Linda Flowers: I always look at the past and try to think where are we going in the future? As a designer and as somebody who wants to put my stamp on things, I submit photos for changes for some of these characters to try to show that... We transformed Flash, Tony [Revoli], on this show. We bleached out the top of his hair and made him look a little hipper. They started out kind of as geeks, and now they're evolving and growing up and finding their place in life. I wanted to help tell that story through their hair.

What was your biggest challenge on this film?
Linda Flowers: The biggest challenge hair-wise was the fact that this movie starts off exactly where the other one left. So there was a lot of direct matching. That's the hardest because people go away. They do other movies. They change their hair. They grow up...

Outside of that, I would say just trying to keep it straight when you have all three Spideys and their doubles. There were eight of them riding around in their suits, and you could be trying to touchup one and it was the wrong one!

How much did you want to update the characters from the earlier movies?
Linda Flowers: We had to change them a little because obviously there's been a huge timeframe in real life. That was many years ago for some of them, and they've aged. Their hair has changed dramatically; and everything has changed. So we tried to do a version of what they would be like if they had aged a little. We tried to find a place in the middle that was believable.

Their performances did not skip a beat. Alfred and Willem were just amazing. They were so physical and brought all the energy and the intensity into it.

What impact does it have on the hair when one of the Spider-Men pulls off his mask?
Linda Flowers: We just put a lot of product in. That's the only thing you can do. And then you always prep them. I always tell them, "When you pull that mask off, if you feel like your hair feels bad, run your fingers through it." No one's ever gonna be upset if he pushes it out of his face or something because that's a natural movement that a normal person would do... Never ever go in front of camera looking bad. I don't care if you're Spider-Man!

What was it like to collaborate with Jon Watts?
Linda Flowers: Working with Jon was great. He was very involved in the look, and I like that... And he would ▶

▶ kinda throw these things at us that would surprise me. Even with a background person, he would want us to do something fun and funky with her hair. I thought, "OK, it's on! He's open to this."

He had a lot on his plate, but he always had a moment to talk to you about the look. He understood that what[ever] goes on, eventually it comes down to the close-up. That's where we get to shine and get our five minutes of fame.

COSTUMES

Does creating costumes for Super Hero movies differ from creating costumes for regular movies?
Sanja Hays: Everything is different. First of all, in this kind of movie, you're building on a tradition of the previous movies, which makes it easier and more

difficult. You have to follow what's been done. You see what they've done well and maybe what could've been improved. But then you don't have so much freedom. It's different, obviously, following somebody else's work. There is building on a Super Hero, on the comics, on the lead of Marvel Studios. So much is at stake.

Did you watch the earlier movies as part of your research?
Sanja Hays: Of course. Then I spent a lot of time pulling pictures and looking through the characters… It was a really looking at what was special and different from one another in [terms of] colors and fashion with Spider-Man and the [other] Super Heroes. Once we settled in and knew what we are doing then it was the question of staying true to what it was in the previous movies and yet making it appealing for the audience of 2021. We tried to change it and adjust it in such a way that it didn't look like a change.

Making the Spider-Man suit has got to be complicated!
Sanja Hays: It's incredibly complicated. It's very difficult to make a pattern because it's not like making the pattern for jeans. Every one of these fabrics is stretchy, so you always have to take into account how much the fabric is gonna stretch. Then once you print the web or design, the whole fabric is printed. It loses the stretch or the stretch becomes different, so you have to take that into account. It's an incredibly precise process.

Every costume has many pieces. Of course, the expectations are that when they put it on that it's gonna be perfect. And it was! But [for] the people that were making them, it [requires] an incredible precision and focus to be able to do that. Then there's the position of where the zippers are so that they don't show, and doing it in such a way that they can take off at least the gloves so they can handle the food and go to the bathroom and talk. Most people just think that he's wearing a unitard, but it's much more than that! ▶

01 Spider-Man unmasked!

02 Ned Leeds.

03 The inside out variation of the Spider-Man suit.

04

► **Was the mask intricate too?**
Sanja Hays: The mask has a skull cap underneath that is molded to his head. That skullcap is actually keeping the shape, of the ears and everything. So he is not wearing the mask just over his bare head. It's intricate to make it as tight as possible, not to add to any of the volume of the skull. We had a special costume when he is without the mask. We called it a "turtleneck costume" and the separate mask kind of goes in.

How did the eyes of the costume work?
Sanja Hays: All the masks had a frame for the eyes to literally snap into. There were different kinds of eyes, depending on how much they had to see and how much the camera had to see and all of that. But when there's movement, that's usually visual effects.

Doc Ock's tentacles were created with visual effects. How did you allow for that in the costume?
Sanja Hays: His belt/girdle or whatever you want to call it was completely practical. It was made out of quite light material. He was always wearing that. Then in the back with his arms, we simply made the holes on the costume that the arms burst out [of]. In those circles, we covered it with the blue screen so it allowed them to put the arms in.

How did the stunts affect your builds?
Sanja Hays: I always think about that. Are they going to be able to move? What's going to happen when they fall? Are they going to be able to put the harness underneath? Sometimes even when we build vests, it's fairly soft until you hit it. Then it becomes hard. They make stunt pads, so sometimes we just line the vests completely with that material so that they don't have to wear additional pads for the stunts. It's part of engineering of every costume.

How closely did you collaborate with the actors?
Sanja Hays: I always talk to them. I try to always be there for them. This is a challenging process. People have no idea how difficult this is to do for actors. There is a reason why they choose the best actors for these movies because they have to stay in character despite of all the physical challenges. It's like, "Oh, now you hang here, now you hang here, then move there." But through all of the endless technical stuff, you have to stay in character… It's part of our job to help them be as comfortable as possible so that they don't have to, as much as possible, think about costume, think about if the shoe is too small, if this is too tight, all of that.

MAKEUP

Is there a different approach for a threequel in terms of makeup?
Vasilios Tanis: Continuity is paramount. When we're doing a film such as this, we have pretty much every photograph ever taken on every *Spider-Man* movie. Especially with this one, we had a lot of matching to do, being that it takes place right after the second one. It's a direct cut, so we had to study all the continuity photos, make sure that everything was proper as far as our actors were concerned... I watched the other films in sequence from beginning to end just to brush up. I'm a big Marvel fan anyway, so it wasn't a big deal for me!

How did you create a fresh look while keeping the original movies in mind?
Vasilios Tanis: There is a time factor as far as when those other movies were shot. So we had to take some liberties as far as having people look as they do and just make them look as best as they possibly could, but also slightly more towards the storyline for some of them. Some of them look a little bit more weathered than others, and that's deliberate. So there was that factor - just looking at the script and seeing what was going on with a character at that particular moment in time.

We depended a lot on lighting and also making sure that facial hair was kept at a certain length, because that has an aging factor on you, especially if the lighting isn't as dark or as light as it can be. We pretty much kept everybody fresh looking, made sure they weren't too matte, and tried to keep them as youthful as possible. We got them on really good skincare regimes prior to shooting, which everybody was excited about!

04 Doctor Strange wearing the Cloak of Levitation.

05 Ned and MJ.

06 Tom Holland shows off the makeup designed to make him look wounded from his fight.

How does the makeup help actors find their character?
Vasilios Tanis: I'm the last step before they get onto the set, and it kind of makes them fall into their character a little bit more with the specific makeup application... It's a collaborative thing between wardrobe, hair, and makeup. The three of us usually work together to create the look for the character, and, of course, the actor's input is very important. We have to make them feel comfortable as well as portraying what we need to portray, as far as having that character coming across the correct way. It's a great process to be involved with. You can tell you're doing your job effectively when they see themselves in the mirror and they're like, "That's it!"

How did you makeup Tom Holland for the fight sequences?
Vasilios Tanis: There were contacts made for him to make him look like even more battered. I feel whenever you get a contact in to create a battered effect it sells it so much more. You really believe it. When you're in the audience, you're like, "Oh my god, that looks horrible!" Wounds are always discussed with the director to see where they're placed.

What was your biggest challenge?
Vasilios Tanis: The biggest challenge was getting a prosthetic piece for Willem Dafoe's character because he has a split personality. With one personality, his teeth look a certain way and then in another, they're completely different. Being that we were in Covid and lockdown, things were a little more complicated. Having something as simple as getting a dental mold fitted and a dental piece constructed was a little challenging considering everybody was spread out all over the world. I was fortunate to have a great support team to help me. 🕷

01

JON WATTS

After masterfully blending high school comedy, heartfelt drama, and spectacular action in *Homecoming* and *Far From Home*, director Jon Watts has made his most ambitious movie yet with *No Way Home*. He gives us an insight into how the movie came together.

02

How did you feel when you saw Sam Raimi's first Spider-Man movie back in 2002?
I loved Sam Raimi before *Spider-Man*. *Evil Dead* and *Evil Dead II* were such huge influences. As a young filmmaker, you're seeing someone do something that is so entertaining and so full of life and comedy and energy and blood. There was something that always felt really approachable about his films where it's like, "I could maybe try to do something like that."

When did the idea to bring back the earlier incarnations of Spider-Man first arise?
I don't remember where the idea started. But just talking through it, it was like, "That would be crazy. That's impossible. How do we do it?" To me, actually, even before it became any sort of multi-versal crossover thing, it was the idea of telling a story that wasn't about being competitive. The idea that it's not about which one's best… The idea that there was maybe some other way of thinking about that. That in a way they are all the same thing, and they could all come together and help each other, trying to figure out what that story might be. That, to me, felt like it was part of the DNA of the story that we were already trying to tell. That gave me an entry point for how to actually get them together so that it was a story element and an emotional thing and not just a gimmick or a series of cameos.

Do you feel like you completed their character arcs in some ways?
Well, both of those franchises had unresolved things. I liked the idea that they show up helping Peter to complete his arc and to make the right decision, and maybe not make the mistakes that they made. But along the way, they get some closure as well, and some catharsis on their storylines.

How did you approach incorporating their stories into the wider story of Tom Holland's Spider-Man?
What's nice about making a movie with three Spider-Men is that you can just ask the Spider-Men what they would do. "What would you be thinking? How would you carry this through?" So a lot of it was collaborative in that way. We just sort of got out folding chairs, and it would be me and Tom and Andrew and Tobey and Z and Jacob, sitting in a circle talking through the story and trying to discover it together and find the nuance. It wasn't like you sit down at your computer, print out the page, and say, "This is what you're gonna say." It meant so much to everyone there that I just wanted to really discover it with them. It became this like really cool - surreal, is the word I keep coming back to - collaborative process.

Did you want to introduce the earlier Spider-Men in a way that people weren't expecting?
What's amazing about the internet is that [if] people have any sort of clue about what might happen, suddenly you get amazing art being generated. People are just posting their ideas for the poster or [asking] "What it would look like if the three of them crossed over?" To me, that was a challenge – just to think like, "What is no one expecting the moment where Tobey and Andrew enter the movie to be?" And that's when I thought of Ned's grandma's house. No one was posting [about] that on their Instagram fan art accounts.

01 Director Jon Watts lines up a shot.

02 Spider-Man snags Spider-Man!

03 Avoiding a low-flying car, as Doc Ock battles the wall-crawler.

Would you say that *No Way Home* is part of Peter Parker's origin story?

For me, I thought it would be really interesting getting to this movie and looking back on what we've done and what we haven't done. The idea that we used three movies to tell Spider-Man's origin story. In Andrew's movie and Tobey's movies, that's the first 40 minutes of the movie. We took three movies to do that. So weirdly, by the end of this movie, we've told the Peter Parker origin story.

That origin story is not just about loss. It's about guilt and shame associated with the loss, the idea that Uncle Ben died and it was because of Peter's selfishness. Peter didn't stop the robber who eventually ended up killing Uncle Ben. And that guilt that he carries with him, that weight is what makes him who he is... And we never really talked about Uncle Ben in the MCU version. In *Captain America: Civil War*, he has a couple lines that sort of dance around the idea, but we felt like that without actually going through that and seeing it, it's not really an origin story yet. So that was fun for me to be able to actually tell that story finally.

Did you want the three Spider-Men to have very distinct ways of moving?

It was fun to look at all of the movies and see what their moves are, because they all have their sort of signature poses and signature moves. That ties in not just to them as actors but also who the stunt coordinators were on those movies and who some of their stunt doubles were on those movies. So we tried to bring back as many people as we could to really be able to delineate who's who.

How did everyone work on developing the dynamics of the different Spider-Men?

I talked to everyone separately at great length - just sort of broad strokes about, "This is what I'm thinking for the characters. And this is the kind of journey we want to be on."

Behind the scenes, they got to actually talk to each other about their experiences as young actors plucked to play this role. They all have that shared experience. So I think it was actually really nice for all of them, as well, to finally be able to talk to someone.

How did it feel to see the three Spider-Man actors in the same movie?

I knew that whatever happened it would be really interesting to see these three guys together! It would at least be an amazing document of a very strange thing that happened.... They're all so good, and I've been so lucky to work with so many incredible actors in a very short amount of time in these movies. To have those three brilliant guys together, and having fun, it was a dream.

Can you talk a little about how you approached the villains?

To me, it was just thinking about what would be fun to see - visual combinations that you never thought you would see. And just at the heart of it, who are these guys? Who are these actors? How great would it be to see Alfred Molina again and Willem Dafoe? And you get to see Willem Dafoe without the mask - really get to see him be who he is. And having Jamie get to come in. ▶

03

04 Spider-Man takes on the Cloak of Levitation.

> ## "To me it was just thinking about what would be fun to see - visual combinations that you never thought you would see."

There's so many great actors that have been in these movies. To be able to bring them all together and to find a way to finish their storylines in a different way... They're all sort of the victims of accidents. They're the victims of technological mistakes, some hubristic, some purely accident. Jamie Foxx just falls into a tank of electric eels. It's just an accident. But to use that as an entry point to tell a story about the idea of second chances...It's like you sort of stumble around with the pieces that you pull together until you find a way to put it together into a story that makes sense.

There's a great scene with the villains in the cells in the basement.
I love the idea of putting a bunch of rogue villains together and just watching them meet each other and hang out and talk. It doesn't necessarily have to be an action scene every time. I love the idea of Sandman and Electro talking about how they got the way they were. I haven't really seen that before.

The film gives us an opportunity to see their individual takes.
There was a nice gray area to explore there. The thing that Peter has been learning is that it's always more complicated than he thinks. In *Homecoming*, he's like, "But that's wrong!" So, to him, it's growing up. Things seem so clearly black or white, and then you start to

04 Spider-Man takes on the Cloak of Levitation.

05 Spidey takes the train as he tries to steal the spell that has trapped the villains.

realize that there's a lot of complexity to issues. And for Peter to get to this place where he's like, "Yes, these guys are bad guys. But why? What happened? Is there something I can do about that?" As opposed to just fighting them and killing them...

It's more just about that fundamental idea that "with great power comes great responsibility" [that] Peter's trying to use to do the right thing. It's his mistake that leads to these guys being here. It's his selfishness and inability to decide between what he wants and where his destiny is taking him. It gets back to that fundamental Spider-Man storyline, which is his selfishness leads to a significant loss, which leads to him realizing that he has to use his power in a responsible way.

Why did you decide to include Doctor Strange?
Like this huge thing is out, and what could he possibly do to try and fix things? I mean, they went to space together... It's a fun thing to sort of sit down and see who Peter knows, see what he would be thinking. Like, what is this 17-year-old kid's solution to this problem? He'd be like, "Well, I know Doctor Strange. Maybe I could ask him for help..."

I mean, if you really think about what Peter's been through, the things that he's seen, what he's experienced, and how closely tied Strange is to all of that... You know, it was basically Strange's idea about how to actually stop Thanos in *Endgame*. That directly leads to the loss of Peter's mentor right in front of his eyes. So it's no stretch of the imagination for me to think that Strange would want to help him.

How important is the chemistry between Peter, MJ, and Ned to the films?
They have that chemistry, and they're genuine friends in real life. And I just love their dynamic, so I wanted to keep that alive, definitely.

It's great that they all went through it together. Not unlike three Spider-Man meeting and finally having someone to talk to, the three of them went through this crazy experience together. So they could always sort of lean on each other, help each other out. In the movie, suddenly Peter, MJ, and Ned become the most famous people in the world. There was a little bit of a parallel, I think, [to] what it felt like for the three of them to suddenly be so huge... For all of them to sort of go through this escalation together, it's nice that they had each other.

Would you say that *No Way Home* is a much bigger movie than your two previous Spider-Man films?
To me, it was a story about trying to get into college and what you do after high school. Leaving that smaller world and entering into a bigger one. The stakes are higher because it's Spider-Man. But there always has to be a personal connection for me or something I can relate to. I never thought of it in terms of, "We gotta go big". To me, it was just reminding myself of what it felt like to be about to graduate high school and be nervous about the future. I mean, I moved from a little town in Colorado to New York City, so that was something I could tap right back into.

05

How did you go about planning out the action sequences?
There are so many people involved in designing that stuff. Like, it's me and George [Cottle, second unit director/stunt coordinator] working out stunts and second unit. It's designing the location to facilitate the kind of action that you want to see. It's the board guys coming up with cool stuff for me – [me] pitching something and them sketching it up. It's the pre-viz team. I worked so closely with the pre-viz guys because there was a big chunk of downtime with the pandemic hit. The only people that were working on the movie in that moment were me and all the pre-viz guys. So it was like, "Hey, let's come up with some stuff. You got three Spider-Man. Like let's just brainstorm what you want to see them do together…" You want to see them like they're three lone wolves. So they're not gonna immediately become perfect teammates. They're used to operating on their own, other than Peter who was in the Avengers. But I want to see them screw up at first. And then that starts to become a story element where you're like, "Oh yeah, they have to learn to work together".

Do you view your three *Spider-Man* films as one overarching story?
It was great to just go back to *Homecoming* and *Far From Home* and figure out any other things that we could connect. Because I just want it to be a complete world where you can see things in this movie that are referencing back to things in the first movie, so that in the end it does feel like one story that we've been telling over three movies. 🕷

KEVIN FEIGE & AMY PASCAL

Producers Amy Pascal and Kevin Feige are two of the most important people behind *No Way Home*. Pascal has been a guiding light for the *Spider-Man* movies since 2002, while Marvel Studios' president Feige has overseen the MCU since its inception.

Why has Spider-Man had such an enduring appeal over the decades?
Amy Pascal: There's something about Peter Parker that all of us understand. He makes a lot of mistakes. He is a kid. And the movies are about kindness. They're about what it means to be a good man. Even 20 years ago when we started talking about these movies, he epitomizes the best in all of us. That spoke to me.

Kevin Feige: [It's] the core of the character from the comics… He wasn't a billionaire. He wasn't from outer space. He was a kid in Queens who got these spectacular abilities and wasn't sure what to do with them or how to utilize them. He learned a tough lesson in his early days with those powers that instilled in him a morality going forward.

Amy Pascal: Also, the Spider-Man stories are often times about love and what you have to give up. I think that's really important. Because he's the only one of all these Super Heroes that is constantly finding out that he has to go it alone. He constantly falls in love, and he constantly wants friendships and he constantly has to give all those things up. It's like all of our lives. And so, the humanness of this story always got me.

You both have a long history with the *Spider-Man* movies…
Amy Pascal: It was around '99 or 2000 that we started working on the [first Tobey Maguire] movie. But it took a long time to put the rights together… I was running the studio then, under John [Calley].

Kevin Feige: I was hired by Marvel almost 21 years ago. I swear within my first week, David Koepp's first or second draft for *Spider-Man* was distributed. Within my first week at Marvel, I was in a production office on the Sony lot with legendary producer Laura Ziskin and legendary director Sam Raimi reading through the new draft going, "How did I get so lucky to be sitting here?" I just kept my mouth shut and learned and watched.

Amy Pascal: Half of my adult life and my professional life has been working on Spider-Man movies. I'm pretty lucky.

The idea of hiring a character actor to play a leading man started with Tobey Maguire.
Amy Pascal: Well, you want an actor. And we have done that every time. You default to great acting, default to great talent, not for whatever the hottest thing of the moment is.

Kevin Feige: It was fun seeing a lot of people go, "Who's this guy playing the legendary, iconic Spider-Man?" Then ▶

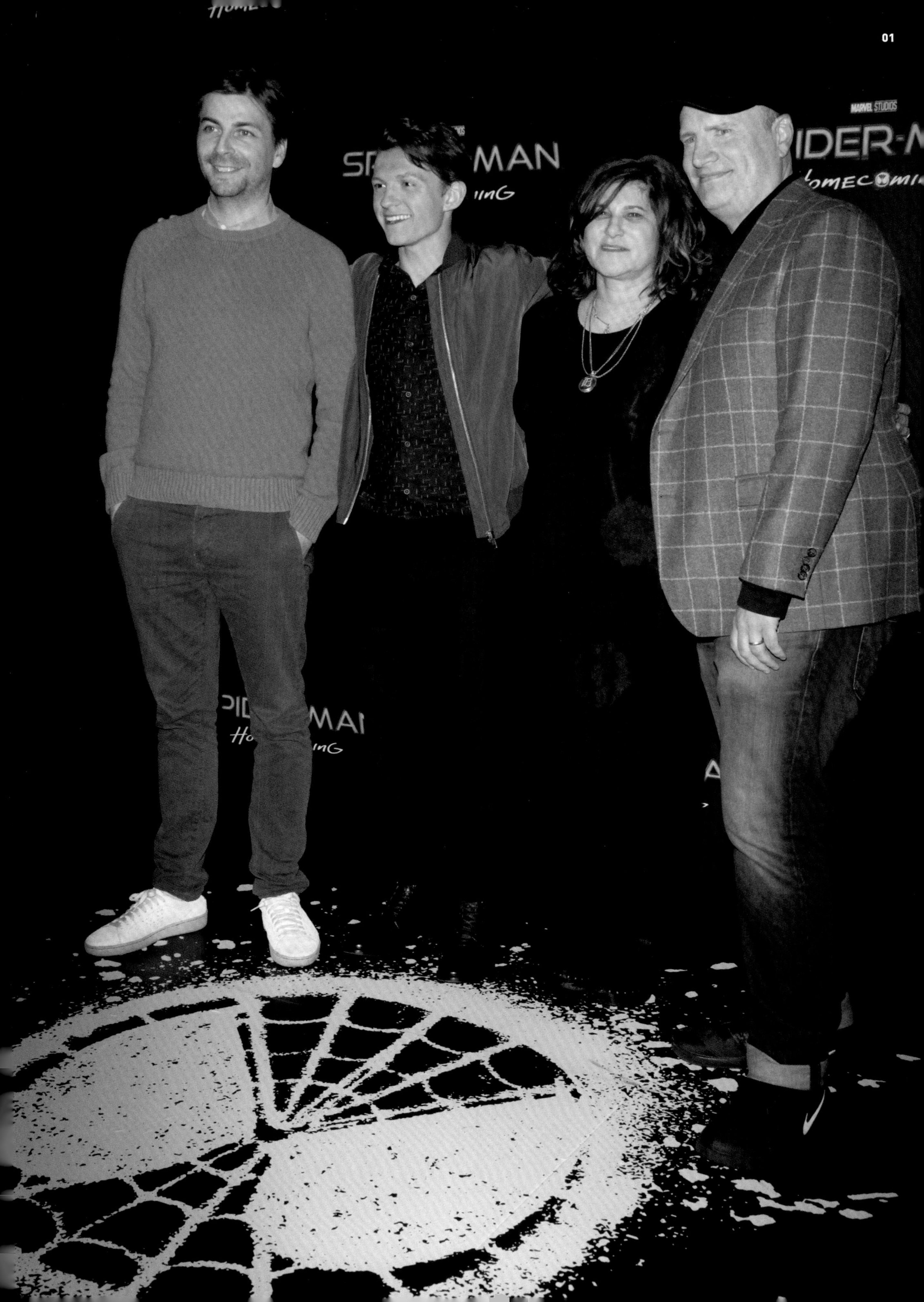
MARVEL STUDIOS

you see the movie and you go, "Oh, he *is* the legendary, iconic Spider-Man."

Amy Pascal: Sam [Raimi] was the visionary of those original movies. He was the one who cast Tobey. We screen-tested him twice to be sure. Of course, by the second screen test we were all in tears, and he blew our mind, as he did for the next 10 years.

Kevin Feige: It's the character that is the marquee value and the actor can become the big superstar name value after that. But it's not about casting whoever was in the number one movie that weekend. It's about finding the soul of the character in a performer, and that's what Sam did with Tobey. That's what we've strived to do on all of our MCU films since.

Andrew Garfield had a slightly different take on the character, didn't he?

Amy Pascal: He had a different interpretation of him than Tobey did. It was edgier... I think that he was a wonderful Spider-Man, and I think the relationship between him and Emma [Stone] was really brilliant. I love those movies. If you go back and look at them now, they're pretty darn good. His performance is amazing. He,

like Tobey, wore Spider-Man pajamas for his entire life. He loves the character. That was one of the great things about being able to do [*No Way Home*] with him.

Can you speak about how the next iteration with Tom Holland developed?

Amy Pascal: Kevin came to see me and said, "You should let me do these movies." I thought about it. And I thought, "You know what? We have to do what's right for Spider-Man. We have to do what's right for that movie...."

We were such good friends. We loved each other. Then I thought about it more, and then I called him a couple weeks later. We had dinner, and I said, "What are you thinking really?" And he said, "I'm thinking that Tony Stark makes him a suit." And, as soon as he said that, I knew I had to do it because I knew that was the right thing to do.

Kevin Feige: When I met with Amy Pascal and first approached her about joining forces to do a Spider-Man movie together and setting it in the MCU, and when we got her blessing and the blessing of Sony and when [Sony Pictures Motion Picture Group chairperson] Tom Rothman came on board and believed in it, there was a lot of pressure, right? There's one thing getting people to say

yes. It's another thing now delivering on what the heck you were talking about.

What did you see in Tom Holland?
Amy Pascal: From the very first second that we saw Tom, he inhabited the character in a way that I don't think any of us had ever seen before. He's a very fine actor as well as an athlete and funny and everything else. But the commitment and passion which he brings to this character and the level of depth which he brings to this character has only increased over the years that we've been making these movies.
Kevin Feige: It became very apparent that Tom Holland was not just an amazing Peter Parker, but he incredibly was an amazing, no pun intended, Spider-Man because he had both the abilities of a great actor and the abilities of a great gymnast and stunt performer. Which was just an added bonus, which continues to blow us away and surprise… There's nothing he can't do.

How did the discussions about *No Way Home* begin?
Kevin Feige: Sitting in a room, in this case it was a conference at Marvel Studios, with the team is always my favorite part of the process where anything is possible. We knew coming out of *Far From Home* that we didn't want to shy away from the fact that his identity is now revealed. It's out there, and that was certainly always the starting point. And with [screenwriters] Erik Sommers and Chris McKenna and our director, Jon Watts, and Amy, we sat and just started brainstorming… We had a lot of fun discussions. It's always having a discussion of, "Oh, you know what would be cool…?"

How did it feel to see the three iterations of Spider-Man in the same movie?
Kevin Feige: Seeing the interaction and the respect between Tobey Maguire and Andrew Garfield and Tom Holland was really quite special.
Amy Pascal: The reason that it worked is because all those guys inhabited Peter Parker. They inhabited that kindness, that generosity, that raw emotion, that openness. I've never seen three people working together playing the same part in my life. And they fell in love with each other.

> "[Tom Holland] continues to blow us away... There's nothing he can't do."

01 From left: Jon Watts, Tom Holland, Amy Pascal, and Kevin Feige attend an event to promote *Spider-Man: Homecoming*.

02 Spider-Man and Doctor Strange join forces.

03 Benedict Cumberbatch goes before the cameras as Doctor Strange.

▶ Kevin Feige: I've had a lot of moments in my career at Marvel that are chill inducing, and you get goosebumps… Even after I had been on set for a while, it always took me a moment when I first saw the three of them in the monitor together to just take a deep breath, calm down, focus on the work, deliver what we wanted to deliver. But it was remarkable.

Did you know you'd be able to get the actors who had appeared in those earlier movies to sign up for this?
Kevin Feige: We don't ever take casting for granted. We don't ever assume somebody will just take our call or sign up sight unseen. So we always want to sit down, have

a meeting, and share all of our hopes and dreams for the project. We often don't have a script written. We don't have perfect scenes written yet. We have an idea and a hope and a dream. We want to bring people into that dream and to trust that together with their inclusion, we can achieve what we're looking to achieve.

Amy Pascal: I had long-standing relationships with Willem, with Alfred, with Jamie, with Andrew and Tobey, with all of them. It could not be a cash grab. It could not be some useless cameo. It had to matter. They had to have stories. There had to be a reason that they were there because for all of these people… For all the characters, these were defining moments in their career. They were

04 Doctor Strange is temporarily ensnared in Spider-Man's web.

05 Peter faces one of his variant's foes, the Sandman.

> "Seeing the interaction and the respect between Tobey Maguire and Andrew Garfield and Tom Holland was really quite special."

everybody thought the same thing. They were really important villains in their own right, and they didn't want to come back and do something that would lessen what they had done. Nobody wanted to do it unless it was gonna be authentic.

Kevin Feige: I'd been saying for years, long before anybody asked me what I thought, that you can't get better than Alfred Molina as Doc Ock, that stepping into those shoes would be very, very difficult. And it would be fun to find a way, if you were ever gonna bring Doc Ock back, for it to be Alfred Molina. And in early development on this third movie, we realized that thanks to the MCU, there is a way to do that.

What does Jon Watts bring to the *Spider-Man* movies?
Amy Pascal: Jon Watts is everything. This is his vision. This is his movie. He has complete command. The actors love him. The crew loves him. He's a spectacular director... It was *Cop Car* that made us hire him. You could see that he knew how to work with kids and that he knew how to tell stories. And he knew how to tell stories through action. A lot of people think they know how to do that, but they don't.

Kevin Feige: What's such an honor working at Marvel Studios is getting to watch storytellers, whether they're actors, whether they're directors, whether they're writers, whether they're the other creative producers, grow and change and evolve over the years. And Jon Watts is an amazing example of that.
Amy Pascal: Jon Watts said, "I want to do it like a John Hughes movie." That was entirely his idea from the very ▶

not gonna just come and show up and do nothing.
Kevin Feige: We were all very nervous when Tobey and Andrew came in and sat down with us, and we were pitching to them what we wanted this movie to be. Why it would do justice to their incarnations of Peter... I had butterflies in those meetings with Tobey and Andrew, hoping that they would sign up.
Amy Pascal: Tobey hadn't been on a movie set in eight years. He said to me when he left, "I think I like acting again." I mean, that made me feel pretty good.

How did you convince the actors who had played villains in the earlier movies to return?
Amy Pascal: None of it was easy at the time because

beginning. He brings a very grounded sensibility. When we were looking at sets, Jon was always like, "No, down, down, down. It's too big. It's too extravagant. That's not Peter's world. That's not what things would look like if you were Peter Parker."

Kevin Feige: *No Way Home* is by far the most ambitious Spider-Man film ever made, and seeing how he's grown into that role and has gone from an excited newcomer to an excited expert has been fun to watch. He handles these tremendous action scenes with a skill that other filmmakers are looking up to and wanting to learn from.

Amy Pascal: As good as he is at the action, and he's great, he's an actor's director too. He really cares about the intimate relationships and the truth of what would be going on between these characters and coming to the emotion from a really honest place.

How has the character of Peter Parker and Spider-Man grown over the films?

Amy Pascal: I've been working with Kevin on Spider-Man movies for the last 20 years. When we started, we were dealing just with the characters that were part of the Spider-Man universe. And one of the great things about the partnership with Marvel and Kevin and the MCU and this whole world, is that we get to continue to tell stories about Spider-Man from Spider-Man's perspective set in a bigger universe... I think that that's been an opportunity for us to show people how different Peter Parker's very humble, ordinary life is. I think you can understand it even better in this larger universe than you can when he's just in his own universe.

Despite the spectacular action scenes, *No Way Home* is a very character-orientated movie.

Amy Pascal: This is definitely 100% the biggest movie that we've ever made. It does take place on a different scale... But the truth is, as much as you have to do that, if the stories aren't intimate, they don't work at all - not with a *Spider-Man* movie. They have to all be about what Peter's dilemma is. So the balance has been to maintain the big action set pieces with the emotion of the character.

Kevin Feige: When you get to a third act battle in any film you want it to be satisfying. You want it to surpass what has come before in the movie, but that doesn't always necessarily mean making things bigger or [saying], "Let's have 10 explosions this time." It's more about the explosion of creativity and emotion within the sequence. And there is a lot of that in the finale of *No Way Home*... It's a level of emotion, I think, that rivals the level of spectacle. That said, when you have five-plus villains, three-plus heroes, MJ, Ned, and Doctor Strange in the mix, it's very, very big!

Amy Pascal: That night on the stage when they were saying goodbye to each other, the three guys, I burst into tears because it was like your whole life. I feel like they were my three sons through different periods of my life... This character moves me in a way that very few things do. ✖

06

07

06 Holland, as Spider-Man, races into action.

07 Spider-Man prepares to tackle Electro.

08 Filming Spider-Man's escape with the box containing Doctor Strange's spell.

08

MARVEL STUDIOS LIBRARY

MOVIE SPECIALS
- MARVEL STUDIOS' *SPIDER-MAN FAR FROM HOME*
- MARVEL STUDIOS' *ANT-MAN AND THE WASP*
- MARVEL STUDIOS' *AVENGERS: ENDGAME*
- MARVEL STUDIOS' *AVENGERS: INFINITY WAR*
- MARVEL STUDIOS' *BLACK PANTHER* (COMPANION)
- MARVEL STUDIOS' *BLACK WIDOW*
- MARVEL STUDIOS' *CAPTAIN MARVEL*
- MARVEL STUDIOS: THE FIRST TEN YEARS
- MARVEL STUDIOS' *THOR: RAGNAROK*
- MARVEL STUDIOS' *AVENGERS: AN INSIDER'S GUIDE TO THE AVENGERS' FILMS*

MARVEL STUDIOS' BLACK WIDOW: THE OFFICIAL MOVIE SPECIAL

MARVEL STUDIOS' THE FALCON AND THE WINTER SOLDIER: THE OFFICIAL MARVEL STUDIOS COLLECTOR SPECIAL

MARVEL STUDIOS' WANDAVISION THE OFFICIAL MARVEL STUDIOS COLLECTOR SPECIAL

MARVEL LEGACY LIBRARY

MARVEL'S AVENGERS BLACK PANTHER: WAR FOR WAKANDA: THE ART OF THE EXPANSION

MARVEL'S CAPTAIN AMERICA: THE FIRST 80 YEARS

MARVEL: THE FIRST 80 YEARS

MARVEL'S DEADPOOL: THE FIRST 60 YEARS

MARVEL'S FANTASTIC FOUR: THE FIRST 60 YEARS

MARVEL CLASSIC NOVELS
- **WOLVERINE** WEAPON X OMNIBUS
- **SPIDER-MAN** THE DARKEST HOURS OMNIBUS
- **SPIDER-MAN** THE VENOM FACTOR OMNIBUS
- **X-MEN AND THE AVENGERS** GAMMA QUEST OMNIBUS
- **X-MEN** MUTANT EMPIRE OMNIBUS

NOVELS
- **MARVEL'S GUARDIANS OF THE GALAXY** NO GUTS, NO GLORY
- **SPIDER-MAN MILES MORALES** WINGS OF FURY
- **MORBIUS** THE LIVING VAMPIRE: BLOOD TIES
- **ANT-MAN** NATURAL ENEMY
- **AVENGERS** EVERYBODY WANTS TO RULE THE WORLD

- **AVENGERS** INFINITY
- **BLACK PANTHER** WHO IS THE BLACK PANTHER?
- **CAPTAIN AMERICA** DARK DESIGNS
- **CAPTAIN MARVEL** LIBERATION RUN
- **CIVIL WAR**
- **DEADPOOL** PAWS
- **SPIDER-MAN** FOREVER YOUNG
- **SPIDER-MAN** KRAVEN'S LAST HUNT
- **THANOS** DEATH SENTENCE
- **VENOM** LETHAL PROTECTOR
- **X-MEN** DAYS OF FUTURE PAST
- **X-MEN** THE DARK PHOENIX SAGA
- **SPIDER-MAN** HOSTILE TAKEOVER

ART BOOKS
- *THE GUARDIANS OF THE GALAXY* THE ART OF THE GAME
- MARVEL'S AVENGERS: *BLACK PANTHER: WAR FOR WAKANDA* THE ART OF THE EXPANSION
- MARVEL'S *SPIDER-MAN MILES MORALES* THE ART OF THE GAME
- MARVEL'S *AVENGERS* THE ART OF THE GAME
- MARVEL'S *SPIDER-MAN* THE ART OF THE GAME
- MARVEL *CONTEST OF CHAMPIONS* THE ART OF THE BATTLEREALM
- *SPIDER-MAN: INTO THE SPIDER-VERSE* THE ART OF THE MOVIE
- THE ART OF IRON MAN THE ART OF THE MOVIE

STAR WARS LIBRARY

STAR WARS: THE MANDALORIAN GUIDE TO SEASON ONE

STAR WARS: THE MANDALORIAN GUIDE TO SEASON TWO

STAR WARS: THE EMPIRE STRIKES BACK: THE 40TH ANNIVERSARY SPECIAL EDITION

STAR WARS INSIDER: THE FICTION COLLECTION VOLUME 2

STAR WARS: THE SKYWALKER SAGA THE OFFICIAL COLLECTOR'S EDITION

- *ROGUE ONE: A STAR WARS STORY* THE OFFICIAL COLLECTOR'S EDITION
- *ROGUE ONE: A STAR WARS STORY* THE OFFICIAL MISSION DEBRIEF
- *STAR WARS: THE LAST JEDI* THE OFFICIAL COLLECTOR'S EDITION
- *STAR WARS: THE LAST JEDI* THE OFFICIAL MOVIE COMPANION
- *STAR WARS: THE LAST JEDI* THE ULTIMATE GUIDE
- *SOLO: A STAR WARS STORY* THE OFFICIAL COLLECTOR'S EDITION
- *SOLO: A STAR WARS STORY* THE ULTIMATE GUIDE
- THE BEST OF *STAR WARS INSIDER* VOLUME 1

- THE BEST OF *STAR WARS INSIDER* VOLUME 2
- THE BEST OF *STAR WARS INSIDER* VOLUME 3
- THE BEST OF *STAR WARS INSIDER* VOLUME 4
- *STAR WARS:* LORDS OF THE SITH
- *STAR WARS:* HEROES OF THE FORCE
- *STAR WARS:* ICONS OF THE GALAXY
- *STAR WARS:* THE SAGA BEGINS
- *STAR WARS* THE ORIGINAL TRILOGY
- *STAR WARS:* ROGUES, SCOUNDRELS AND BOUNTY HUNTERS
- *STAR WARS:* CREATURES, ALIENS, AND DROIDS
- *STAR WARS: THE RISE OF SKYWALKER* THE OFFICIAL COLLECTOR'S EDITION

- *STAR WARS: THE MANDALORIAN:* GUIDE TO SEASON ONE
- *STAR WARS: THE MANDALORIAN:* GUIDE TO SEASON TWO
- *STAR WARS: THE EMPIRE STRIKES BACK* THE 40TH ANNIVERSARY SPECIAL EDITION
- *STAR WARS: AGE OF RESISTANCE* THE OFFICIAL COLLECTORS' EDITION
- *STAR WARS: THE SKYWALKER SAGA* THE OFFICIAL COLLECTOR'S EDITION
- *STAR WARS INSIDER: FICTION COLLECTION* VOLUME 1
- *STAR WARS INSIDER PRESENTS: MANDALORIAN SEASON 2* VOLUME 1
- *STAR WARS INSIDER PRESENTS: MANDALORIAN SEASON 2* VOLUME 2

AVAILABLE AT ALL GOOD BOOKSTORES AND ONLINE

TITAN-COMICS.COM | TITANBOOKS.COM